Inspiring Active Learning

A Handbook for Teachers

Merrill Harmin

Association for Supervision and Curriculum Development
Alexandria, Virginia

Association for Supervision and Curriculum Development
1250 N. Pitt St., Alexandria, VA 22314.
Telephone: (703) 549-9110. Fax: (703) 549-3891 or 836-7921.

Printed in the United States of America.
Cover and interior design by Karen Monaco.

Ronald S. Brandt, *Executive Editor*
Nancy Modrak, *Managing Editor, Books and Editorial Services*
Julie Houtz, *Senior Associate Editor*
Gary Bloom, *Manager, Design and Production Services*
Stephanie Kenworthy, *Production Coordinator*
Karen Monaco, *Senior Graphic Designer*
Valerie Sprague, *Desktop Publishing Specialist*

ASCD Stock No.: 1-94027
Price: $14.95
ISBN: 0-87120-228-X

Library of Congress Cataloging-in-Publication Data

Harmin, Merrill.
    Inspiring active learning : a handbook for teachers / Merrill Harmin.
        p.   cm.
    Includes bibliographical references and index.
    ISBN 0-87120-228-X
    1. Teaching—Handbooks, manuals, etc.   2. Motivation in education—
Handbooks, manuals, etc.   3. Active learning—Handbooks, manuals,
etc.   I. Title.
LB1025.3.H37   1994
371.'02—dc20   93-49379
                                                                   CIP

This work is dedicated to Grace H. Pilon, a true educational genius and the creator of the WORKSHOP WAY® instructional design. It was from her I learned many of the strategies that are most effective with today's students. Although my adaptation of her strategies does not necessarily represent her intentions, I most graciously give credit to Pilon for the following strategies in this book: Ask a Friend, Truth Signs, Cushioning, Plain Corrects, Plain Incorrects, Intelligence Call Up, Once Principle, Student Procedure Mastery, Homework Hearing, Pass the Q&A, and What's the Difference?

Inspiring Active Learning: A Handbook for Teachers

RAISING STUDENT MOTIVATION

ORGANIZING THE CLASSROOM

Foreword

Schools today face a formidable antagonist: societal conditions that work against students, impeding their academic growth and preventing them from carrying into the world beyond the school the skills and concepts taught in the classroom. Schools have always had as their goal the extension of learning beyond school time and beyond the school years. Just how to accomplish this and develop productive, responsible citizens is one of the much-debated issues in education today. If education is a social investment—and it is—then teaching students how to live in society after they leave the school culture is one of the best ways to make that investment pay off. Merrill Harmin offers hope for achieving this goal through his approach to developing a classroom that steadfastly promotes dignity, energy, self-management, community, and awareness.

Inspiring Active Learning: A Handbook for Teachers takes the long view of education, sees students as citizens of tomorrow, and attempts to prepare them to assume that role. The book presents tested practices that address the needs of the whole child. It is brimming with ideas that help teachers inspire students to take charge of their learning. Students are not merely the passive recipients of knowledge; they are constantly shaping their lives as they learn, being empowered to develop the best they have within them. Without detracting from the academic agenda, these strategies imbue the classroom with a new spirit. In fact, a classroom in which students value themselves and respect one another, and a classroom in which students are expected to be reasonable in their actions, creates an atmosphere that is most conducive to learning.

One of the most noteworthy aspects of this book is that it is a collection of strategies culled from practicing teachers in various schools and in different stages of their professional lives. It is encouraging that such strategies are being applied in classrooms and that students today are benefiting from this approach to teaching and learning. With its novel organization and practical approach, this book will help make these strategies permanent practices in classrooms across the nation.

BARBARA TALBERT JACKSON
ASCD President, 1993–94

Introduction

This book brings good news to teachers: The profession now has available practical teaching strategies that make it much easier to get today's students to buckle down to their daily work. You will find a sampling of them in this book.

These strategies reduce the need to push and pull at students, struggling to get them to learn. The strategies tend to catch students up naturally in learning. They *inspire* involvement and, in the process, inspire the development of some of the most healthful, constructive potentials students carry. As a result, month by month, students become increasingly mature and responsible, and the classroom increasingly becomes a pleasant, thriving learning community.

The strategies of this book are also quite doable, so teachers can readily test this proposition for themselves. Indeed, no strategy has been included here unless many teachers at all levels of instruction, from kindergarten through college, have already tested it and found it both workable and effective, even in today's pressured classrooms, even with today's restless students. For example, teachers report effectively using the strategies to:

- Increase time-on-task scores for both slow and gifted students.
- Get students at risk to learn in ways that advance responsible self-management.
- Modernize a reading program to meet different learning styles.
- Reduce misbehavior in and out of classrooms.
- Ease the restructuring of a junior high into a middle school.
- Help new teachers get classrooms running smoothly.
- Assist in the implementation of an integrated, outcome-based curriculum.
- Shift attention from extrinsic rewards to intrinsic learning satisfactions.

The instructional strategies of this book are similar to strategies gaining ground in industry: They center on mutual respect, not bossiness; collaboration, not isolation; worker commitment to the job, not fear of failure; and, most essentially, on the dignity of all, not praise and rewards for a few.

Setting a Target

There are two basic ways to use this book:

1. Ease teaching and improve learning. You might start by picking and choosing strategies you are willing to try in your classroom. I recommend beginning with the first chapters, for they contain the strategies most teachers find helpful at the outset. Experiment and see if the strategies help you draw more of your students into active learning more of the time and with less struggle and effort.

2. Aim for a fully inspirational classroom. Once you are clear about this inspiring approach to instruction, as compared to an approach that relies on extrinsic rewards and punishments, you might consider aiming to run a classroom that always inspires all students, even those typically hard to reach. I did not always believe this was a realistic goal. But we have now identified many strategies for inspiring learning—so many that I believe *any* of us, no matter what our grade level or degree of natural charisma, can run an inspirational classroom.

The education profession is now in breakthrough territory. I am convinced that each of us everyday, in every lesson, can draw students toward active, productive learning and, in the process, also draw them toward productive, healthful living. This breakthrough became apparent fairly early in my research into this inspirational approach to instruction and especially after studying teachers who used the WORK-SHOP WAY® strategies of Grace Pilon (1981, 1987, 1991). I visited many teachers she had trained and I witnessed each of them steadily inspiring all students. Even teachers who told me they had recently been close to burnout were doing so—and they were doing so with students usually viewed as nearly unmanageable. I saw no student rewarded, none punished. I heard no scoldings, no putdowns, no teasing, not one negative judgment in a whole school day. Moreover, there was strong evidence that students were steadily growing in self-responsibility, self-respect, and respect for others (Harmin 1990). It became clear that what had long been recommended by educational theorists (Dewey 1916, 1938; Guilford 1967; McLuhan and Fiore 1967) had become technically realistic; now all teachers, even those without special gifts, can learn to run a classroom based on students' healthful intrinsic motives.

A few teachers, of course, have always had the knack of inspiring students to work hard. They have never much needed to push and struggle with students. All of us have had the experience of inspiring *some* of our students. Now we can learn how to inspire *all* of our students. This book aims to demonstrate this possibility.

But let me be more specific. If we wanted to move toward a fully inspirational classroom, a classroom that kept calling forth the best students have in them, what would be our target? Operationally speaking, what would tell us we had succeeded? Surface appearances would not tell us much, for a fully inspirational classroom does not conform to any one standard image. We might see students sitting in traditional rows or we might see students scattered in small groups. Yet we can clearly identify a classroom in which students' most healthful, productive qualities are shining forth. If we visit such a classroom, we will observe high levels of five qualities:

Dignity. We see students looking confident and ready to learn. They sit tall, proud of themselves and their abilities. They appear to have respect for themselves. They do not slouch about as if ashamed, but rather appear to have an inner strength. They feel secure in the classroom and relax and invest themselves unself-consciously in their studies. They are not constantly on guard, worried about pleasing everyone or winning every game, as if their worth as human beings depended on success or praise.

Energy. Students are busy, engaged, involved. The classroom hums with activity. We do not see much waiting, restlessness, or downtime. Students do not watch the clock, impatient for class to end. Nor do students work frantically, anxiously, stressfully, as if they have been whipped into action. They simply work with a comfortable energy.

Self-Management. Students are self-managing and self-motivating. They take responsibility for themselves. They make their own choices, begin and end work on their own, and correct their own work when possible. They don't need detailed orders. It is as if students are saying,

"I'm taking care of what I need to take care of. I can manage. I don't need to be told every little thing."

Community. We see students in comfortable relationships with other students and with persons of authority. Students listen to one another. They are accepting and accepted. They are respectful and respected. They do not tease or slight others. They do not feel isolated, rejected, or disconnected from others. Nor do they become mired in self-centeredness or resentment. Problems may arise, but students and teachers resolve them in ways appropriate to respectful community living. A classroom that brings out the best in students, and in teachers too, encourages students to learn in reasonable community with others, not in isolation, and not in opposition to others.

Awareness. Students are thoughtful and alert; they know what is happening in the classroom. We see concentration, wonderment, creativity, and diligence. Students are not bored; they don't plod through the day with dulled awareness. They do not handle their studies mindlessly. Students are attuned to the dynamics of the classroom, to their own thoughts and feelings, and to the ideas and feelings of the people around them.

Incidentally, this awareness is different from thought, reasoning, or intelligence. Indeed, people who are quite ordinary reasoners are often quite successful in life because they are highly aware. People are not likely to be effective in life, however, if they are not aware of what is going on within and around them. We can be aware of memories, facts, emotions, colors, sounds, ideas, others, and ourselves. We can be aware of future possibilities, as when we consider options for a story ending or our activities tonight. We can even be aware of possibilities not yet perceived by others. And we can choose which awareness to focus on: "Should I continue worrying about what I'm going to do tonight or get back to my book?" A useful definition of intelligence combines our powers of awareness and self-management: We are intelligent, we might say, to the extent we can manage our awareness. If we can open our minds to many awarenesses, and then manage to hold our attention on our selected focus, we are apt to produce results that would be called intelligent.

For convenience, I call these five elements by their first initials, DESCA. I have found that DESCA serves teachers well as a specific yet comprehensive and flexible teaching target. A bull's eye, in this scheme, would be a classroom in which every student handles subject matter with solid dignity, balanced energy, appropriate self-management, community feelings, and focused awareness.

I am most satisfied with my teaching when I see my students working with high DESCA, because students are then studying in a way that is likely to bring out their best and thus further their academic learning now and their long-term living later. When I notice low DESCA, I am less satisfied and look for alternative instructional strategies. What do I mean by low DESCA? Low dignity, for one thing: students getting down on themselves, blaming themselves, losing trust in themselves. Or low energy, as when I sense apathy coloring the class mood. Or low self-management, as when I see students working passively, doing only what they have been told to do, or working without clear personal commitment. Or low community, as when students maliciously tease each other or when I see that some students feel left out. Or low awareness, as when minds cloud over, boredom spreads, or responses become thoughtless and superficial. Even when students seem to be mastering the lesson of the day, I am not satisfied with low DESCA because I am committed to keeping my classroom running as a dignified, energetic, self-managing community of aware learners.

This book can be used as a guide to finding instructional strategies that help you both teach subject matter and inspire students to unfold these five basic human potentials. I've included two forms in the book that can help you experiment with the possibilities of incorporating the idea of DESCA into your classroom. The first, the DESCA Scale for Rating a Class (on page 6), is useful for rating a class you have just taught or are now observing. Some teachers also get students' perception of a class by asking students to fill out this form. Teachers interested in the perspectives of young children may prefer to use the second form, A DESCA Questionnaire (on page 7).

DESCA is certainly not all of what defines a good classroom today. But I believe it covers the heart of it. The many teachers I have worked with tell me it is a useful, flexible, encompassing target. Their reports suggest that as teachers keep tapping into those five human potentials, instructing in ways that stir them into growth, students increasingly sense that teachers are on their side and on the side of the best they have within them.

DESCA Scale for Rating a Class

DIGNITY

| 1 | 2 | 3 | 4 | 5 |

No personal dignity: Students slouch or mope, as if feeling unimportant, weak, or hopeless. Or they act as if they will be worthless without high success or others' approval. Little evidence of self- confidence, self-respect.

Clear dignity in all: Talented or not, students sit and walk tall and speak up. Seem self-assured, confident, secure. Much evidence that students trust themselves and see themselves as valuable persons, worthy of respect.

ENERGY

| 1 | 2 | 3 | 4 | 5 |

Energy too low or high: Mood is slow; students seem lifeless, with much inactivity, apathy, waiting, time wasting. Or energy is too high; students seem stressed, frantic, anxious, frazzled.

Flow of comfortable energy: The mood is vital, active, healthful. All students keep busy, engaged. No evidence of clock-watching. Time seems to fly.

SELF-MANAGEMENT

| 1 | 2 | 3 | 4 | 5 |

Students only follow orders: No evidence of self-responsibility, initiative, self-direction, personal choice. Students work passively, without personal commitment.

All students are self-directing: Students make appropriate choices, guide and discipline themselves, work willingly, with persistence. Students are not bossed.

COMMUNITY

| 1 | 2 | 3 | 4 | 5 |

Students are self-centered: Students act only for personal advantage with little concern for others' welfare. No evidence of teamwork, loyalty, belonging, kindness toward peers or toward teacher.

Strong mood of togetherness: Much sharing, cooperation, interdependence, mutuality. Students support one another and the teacher. No antagonism, rejection.

AWARENESS

| 1 | 2 | 3 | 4 | 5 |

Awareness is dull or narrow: Students seem bored, unaware, unresponsive, shallow. Work is mechanical busywork. No thinking, concentrating, or searching. Student talk is impulsive, uncreative, routine, thoughtless. Much inattentiveness.

All students are aware and alert: Much concentration, observing, listening, thinking, noticing, evaluating. Students appear to be mindful, aware of what is going on. High level of attentiveness.

A DESCA Questionnaire

Dear Student:

How was class for you today? Please check one item in each category.

Dignity

_____ I had strong, good feelings about myself.
_____ I felt pretty positive and secure.
_____ Unsure.
_____ I didn't feel very good about myself.
_____ I thought I was hopeless, bad, or stupid.

Energy

_____ I was comfortably active and energetic all the time.
_____ I was comfortably active and energetic most of the time.
_____ Unsure.
_____ I didn't put much energy into my work.
_____ I felt inactive and low, or anxious and stressed.

Self-management

_____ I made many choices, managed myself, always felt self-responsible.
_____ I was rather self-managing, somewhat self-responsible.
_____ Unsure.
_____ I drifted along, not using much of my own willpower.
_____ I was only controlled or bossed. I was not at all self-responsible.

Community

_____ I felt I belonged in the group. I felt fully accepted.
_____ I had generally positive feelings about others.
_____ Unsure.
_____ I did not feel fully accepted.
_____ I felt only selfishness and rejection from others.

Awareness

_____ I was aware and alert all the time.
_____ I was aware and alert most of the time.
_____ Unsure.
_____ I was often bored and unresponsive.
_____ I paid little attention. I was extremely bored.

The Importance of Setting a Target

You don't have to use DESCA as your target to benefit from the strategies in this book. But do identify a target. Set your priorities, at least temporarily. Don't try to go off in many directions at the same time. When we are heading in one clear direction, we are in the best position to make professional decisions and stick to them. We can say, "I will not do that. That will distract me from my main purpose." It's hard to make such statements when our priorities are unclear. It's hard not to respond to all the demands others would load on us. It's hard not to spin dizzily, getting nowhere. Once you have a clear target that is appropriate for your classroom, you can find your own ways to hit that target more often and more easily with more students.

You might, of course, choose other targets. On the basis of the experiences of other teachers, you can use the strategies in this book to focus on:

- Improving attendance and retention rates.
- Reducing tardiness and increasing attendance and retention rates among students at risk.
- Implementing a portfolio assessment program (or other curriculum reforms).
- Experiencing less stress at the end of a teaching week and more joy on Monday mornings.
- Easing the process of mainstreaming special education students.

Your Own Strategy Package

Once you choose your target, move ahead to creating your own strategy package for meeting that target. When I conduct classes, DESCA is my target. Let's say I teach a class in educational theory. The subject of the class gives me my content. DESCA guides me in developing a process—that is, choosing strategies—to convey that content. That is, the process I develop should then lead to growth in group dignity, energy, self-management, community, and awareness, all of which will allow my class to become better able to learn about educational theory.

You can create a personal strategy package in that way. You can be your own transforming agent. Just be aware of what is happening in the classroom as you teach. If DESCA is your target, perhaps keep a card on your desk: *How am I doing at exercising and advancing dignity, energy, self-management, community, and awareness of all students? Can I do better?* Keep asking questions that relate to your target until they become knee-jerk reactions when you look out on your students. That will lead you to a strategy package that works well for you.

If you choose this path, take your time. Move at a pace that feels right, but stick to the campaign. Almost all teachers bump into old, limiting assumptions and habits along the way. Give yourself time to move past those obstacles. Perhaps also get a support buddy or two. It's much easier to keep at a plan like this when we do not go it alone. And, if DESCA is your target, working together is just a natural part of the community you're striving for. Perhaps risk asking your buddies to observe your teaching and to offer their perceptions and suggestions.

I recommend, too, being clear about your intentions, for it is easy to misuse any educational approach. No matter what your target, consider holding these two intentions: First, intend to master the art of running a classroom that always and steadily serves both subject matter learning and long-term, dignified living for every student. A good start is to adopt the medical pledge "First, do no harm." Second, intend to see every student—no matter how hopeless he or she may appear—as potentially ready, and perhaps ready right now, to leap dramatically ahead. Never give up on a student. None of us can ever be certain when another person is ready to make a major advance. There is more potential in people than most of us know— likely more than they themselves know. Intend to see more of that potential burst forth at any moment. This mind-set lies at the heart of the inspirational approach to teaching. It is really not very complicated or very new. In a way, all we need do is keep appreciating the goodness that lies within every student, however tempted we are to deny that it exists. The teaching strategies in this book will make it easier for you to keep doing this.

The Power of One Teacher

I recently read about a slum neighborhood in Montreal in which violence and decadence were at extremely high levels (see Pedersen, Faucher, and Eaton 1978). In the middle of that neighborhood was an elementary school. Not surprisingly, researchers found that few children who went to that school ever improved their lifestyle. Even after twenty-five years of adulthood, only 29 percent of its graduates had more than menial jobs or lived in reasonably decent housing. Thirty-eight percent of graduates existed at the lowest levels of survival, typically homeless and unemployed.

Some graduates of this elementary school, however, were more successful: specifically, the students who had a 1st grade teacher called "Miss A." The researchers noticed something curious about Miss A's former students. While only 29 percent of the graduates of most teachers broke free of their old lifestyle, a full 64 percent of the students who had Miss A did so. Furthermore, while 38 percent of the students of other 1st grade teachers were found to be living at the lowest levels of poverty, *none* of the students who had Miss A was found living at that level. Clearly, one 1st grade teacher was somehow having a dramatic, long-term effect on her students, doing much more than teaching reading, writing, and arithmetic.

My mind jumps to Marva Collins and Jaime Escalante, two other teachers able to inspire remarkable growth from unpromising students. You can probably think of even more teachers who are able to teach in ways that move students to achieve academic and personal excellence. I believe any of us can now get the same kinds of results. The profession now offers us a sufficient number of tools so we can teach our subject matter while we also help students reveal and express the best that is within them. If you have doubts, I invite you to treat the idea as an interesting possibility, one you can test with the aid of the strategies in this book.

Additional Teaching Strategies

This book contains only a sampling of the strategies we have collected that help teachers fulfill their responsibilities in inspirational ways. If you would like a more complete set or information about on-site demonstration or training programs, please contact me at the address below:

Merrill Harmin
The Inspiration Strategies Institute
105 Lautner Road
Edwardsville, IL 62025
Telephone: (618) 692-0177

1 Strategies for Developing High-Involvement Lessons

The shrinking attention span of today's students makes teaching more difficult than ever. Many teachers have told me that in struggling to capture and hold students' attention, they must be more entertainer than teacher. This does not have to be. It is possible to hold students' attention without putting on a show every day. I recommend you do so through a combination of DESCA, described in the Introduction, and high-involvement lessons, described in this chapter.

High-involvement lessons are exactly what the name implies: lessons that elicit a high level of student involvement. You can achieve high involvement by using four basic strategies:

- Strategy 1.1: Action flow lesson plan
- Strategy 1.2: Quick pace
- Strategy 1.3: Teaching in layers, not lumps
- Strategy 1.4: Limited variety

You'll find that these four strategies work naturally together in the classroom, and that it's hard to separate one from the other and still use them effectively. In describing how they work, I mention other strategies. At this point, it's not important that you understand exactly how those strategies work. They are described more fully in this book.

Strategy 1.1: Action Flow Lesson Plan

Description: A lesson plan organized so the class proceeds smoothly, interestingly, with high student involvement.

Purpose: To get enough action going so students naturally get involved in learning, without needing threats or rewards.

A typical action flow lesson moves at a quick pace. It avoids lulls and, certainly, hints of boredom. Students feel the momentum of the lesson and always have something to do. Pacing is important. The teacher rarely slows down, even when students have not yet mastered the material introduced. Action flow lessons often overlap subject matter from day to day, so students have multiple opportunities to master the material.

An action flow lesson also has plenty of variety. In one lesson there is some of this and some of that, so if *this* does not capture students' attention, perhaps *that* will. You'll typically use several instructional strategies in each lesson, depending on what you want to accomplish. For instance, do you want students to think extra carefully at this point? If so, how do you get them to do that? Do you want students to begin constructing personal meanings? If so, how do you get them to do that? The many teaching strategies in this book should help you meet such different needs.

Here are four examples of action flow lessons. Each will, of course, need to be adjusted to fit different grade levels and subject areas.

Action Flow Lesson 1: Write-Share-Learn

1. The Question, All Write strategy. Pose a question to the class that will make them think. For instance: "What do we all know about planets and stars?" or "What makes for a really good song?" or "How can we tell the difference between a courageous act and a foolish act?" or "What are some ways we can dream up to make mental addition easier?" or "How might we improve the lunch room (or anything of interest to students)?" Chapter 13 includes ideas for questions that naturally generate such thinking.

Ask each student to respond to the question by making some private notes. Ask with confidence, expecting all students will write something down. Don't worry if some do nothing at the outset. You want the "flow" of the action lesson to eventually capture student attention.

2. The Attentive Discussion strategy. When you see that three or four students have finished writing, announce, "Just finish the thought you are now writing." Do not wait until most students finish. Keep the pace upbeat. Students will soon learn it's not important to write everything that they're thinking during this kind of activity.

Tell students you'd like a few of them to share their ideas. Invite responses and discussion by asking who is willing to go first. Don't let the discussion go too long. When you sense that involvement is about to slump, move on. A short discussion that zips along is better than a discussion that drags.

3. The Sharing Pairs strategy. Ask students to pair up with someone nearby and share their thoughts or notes. Let students pick their own partners, helping only those who can't manage. Students need to practice this kind of self-management. (If you haven't already helped students learn how to move into pairs efficiently, you might plan to do so in a future lesson.) Tell students, "You'll have just a few minutes for sharing. Go!" Say "Go!" as if starting a race. Zip up the energy level.

When you see that two or three pairs have finished sharing their ideas, announce: "Just one moment please" or "Just finish the thought you are now on." Then firmly call the class together. Even if some students have barely begun sharing their thoughts about the topic, do not worry. Students will eventually realize that you do not give excess time for small-group talk, and they will learn to move quickly into discussion.

4. The Attentive Lecture strategy. Without waiting for students to be quiet and ready (you want *activity* to catch students up, and *waiting* has nothing active in it), ask: "Who will share something that you or your partner talked about?" This question will usually lead to a discussion you can use as a stepping stone to an Attentive Lecture, as by closing the discussion with something like, "Here are some thoughts I have." Trust the sound of your voice to call to order students who have been slow to disengage from sharing pairs. Do not repeat what you say. Do not frown. Give students the opportunity to learn to meet your quick pace. If you choose to share your ideas, talk only as long as class attention remains high. Move to another strategy when you sense that the attention level is about to drop.

5. Options for proceeding. You may want to use the Question, All Write strategy again: "You may have clarified or changed your ideas by now. Take a moment and make some additional notes to yourself or, if you like, draw something related to what we discussed." Or you may want to return to the Attentive Discussion strategy: "Is anyone willing to share reactions to what we've just heard or willing to share any other ideas you have?" Or you may want to do something else for a bit.

6. The Outcome Sentences strategy. Conclude the lesson by saying: "Please think back over what we have done so far. We began with a question and did some thinking and sharing. See if you can write two or three things you got from what we did so far. You may want to begin your sentences with words like these" [then read aloud the chart you had earlier posted or written on the chalkboard]:

- I learned . . .
- I was surprised . . .
- I'm beginning to wonder . . .
- I rediscovered . . .
- I feel . . .
- I think I will . . .

"See how many conclusions you can get for yourself from this lesson. Go."

When you see that three or four students have stopped writing, alert students that you'll be moving on in just a moment. If you feel it's appropriate, ask if anyone is willing to read aloud one of their outcome sentences.

If time permits, ask students to sit with a partner and take turns sharing one or two things they learned.

Action Flow Lesson 2: Practice-Instruct-Review

A note on the format: Action Flow Lessons 2, 3, and 4 are presented in a format especially valuable for reviewing the flow of action in a lesson. The left column contains (1) the name of the teaching strategy used, (2) the arrangement of the class (e.g., small groups), and (3) the approximate duration of the strategy. The right column contains teaching directions and describes how the strategy should play out.

1. Choral Work
   whole class
   4-6 minutes

Show cards containing math facts, chemical symbols, spelling words, phrases—any material students must internalize. Lead students in chanting each card in rhythm. Turn cards briskly and encourage high energy with "A little more power please."

2a. Guided Practice
   whole class
   3-6 minutes

Pose a problem from yesterday's lesson. While each student works alone at desk, solve problem correctly on board. Students check own work. Focus is on student practice. No expectation is held that all students have mastered the material. Assess content mastery as lesson proceeds. Avoid extended discussion, keep pace moving.

If much confusion:
2b. *Think Aloud*
   whole class
   5-10 minutes

Work some problems aloud after students have tried to solve them. Aim is to model thinking that solves the problem.

Math example: "Since I don't know what to put here, I think I'll try an estimate. I see I need something larger than six because . . . "

Science example: "How should I approach this? How would it work if I . . . Oops, that doesn't work. Let me try . . . "

If understanding is low*:*
3a. *Sharing Pairs*
   5-10 minutes

Tell students to pick a partner and help each other or, if both understand, to create new challenges for each other. Circulate and help students as necessary.

If understanding is high:
3b. Think Aloud
   whole class
   6-12 minutes

Introduce easy example of new problem, thinking aloud while working on the board. Pose a similar problem for students to work at desks, then work that problem on board, again thinking aloud.

Pose a slightly harder problem to students, let them work it, then work it on board. Continue at a comfortable pace. Avoid extended discussions. Handle confusions another day. Move on *before* interest lags.

4. Review Test
   whole class
   4-8 minutes

Write first problem on board. Pause to let students begin working it. Work it correctly on board as students are working. Tell students they are to correct their own work. Proceed through a set of problems. Avoid giving instruction on how to solve problems. Focus is on review, self-correction, and personal challenge. The pace is sufficiently brisk to maximize student involvement.

5. Voting Strategy
   whole class
   1-2 minutes

At end, perhaps give students a few moments to assess their learning process or learning outcomes and to express themselves by asking: "How many did some good risking on today's review test? How many strengthened old understandings? How many like the way they handled today's review test?" Students respond by raising hands. With this strategy it's no grades, no rewards, no slights.

Action Flow Lesson 3: Cushioning-Underexplain-Learning Pairs

1. Cushioning
   whole class
   1-2 minutes

Reduce student anxiety and maximize relaxed, open-minded attentiveness: "We will talk about something new today. Do not assume you need to understand it completely right now. We will review and help each other later, so relax and let's just see what happens today."

2. Underexplain with
   Learning Pairs
   5-15 minutes

Present a concept or principle (e.g., "There are lots of ways to get a scale like this to balance. You can move this center point or the position of the weights, as I am doing here. You can invent your own system, but one general rule to follow is . . . ") Continue brief, cursory explanation, so perhaps only half the class understands it. Then say:

"Now get together in pairs. Help each other figure out how to do this. When you both get it, work some practice problems. If you're both stuck, ask another pair for help."

3. Attentive Lecture/ Discussion
whole class
time as appropriate

"How did we do? What did you figure out? What questions remain?" Continue discussion or explanation as appropriate, but no longer than whole-class involvement and attention are maintained.

4. Ask a Friend
individual work
time as appropriate

"Now, please complete your worksheets. Practice good thinking. If you get stuck, ask a friend for help."

Action Lesson Plan 4: Lecture-Share-Learn

1. Speak-Write
whole class
2-5 minutes

Lecture until reaching a natural break in the material, but not more than 5 minutes. Then say: "Take a moment and write the key ideas you've heard so far or any questions you have."

2. Working Alone
1-2 minutes

Students write. When three or four students have finished writing, say "One more moment please."

3. Speak-Write
whole class
3-5 minutes

Continue lecture to next natural break point, but not so long that students cannot hold the material comfortably in mind. Then say: "Now I want you to make some notes again about what you heard or questions you have about what I just said."

Continue this speak-write sequence as appropriate, ending before you start losing students' attention.

4. Sharing Pairs
2-8 minutes

Ask students to form pairs and share a summary of what they heard, what they think are important points, or questions that occurred to them.

5. Lecture Summary whole class *2-5 minutes*	"Let me summarize what I would most like you to understand, what I see as the main points . . . "
6. Attentive Discussion whole class *time as appropriate*	"Who would be willing to share ideas or reactions or questions?"
7. Outcome Sentences individual *2-4 minutes*	Ask students to review lesson, make note of key things they learned, rediscovered, or perhaps are now wondering about.
9. Whip Around, Pass Option whole class time as appropriate	"Starting at this wall, let's whip around part of the class. When it comes your turn, read one of your 'I learned' statements or, if you prefer, say 'I pass.' "

These four lesson plans are meant only to suggest how an action flow lesson typically proceeds. They may not be suitable for every teacher or for every class. The test for any action flow plan is straightforward: How well does it produce a lesson that draws all students into a learning activity and how well does it keep students engaged throughout the lesson? Lesson plans like this are not new. The first plan, for instance, is similar to the "Think, Pair, Share" series developed by Frank Lyman at the University of Maryland (McTighe and Lyman 1988) and the second is similar to the "guided practice" step of Barak Rosenshine's (1979, 1983) direct instruction model.

Strategy 1.2: Quick Pace ──────────────────────

Description: A classroom pace fast enough to keep all students actively involved.

Purpose: To prevent students' attention from wandering.

Life seems to be speeding along nowadays, and students seem to have internalized that fast pace. Few have patience for the slow and deliberate. In my experience, students usually stay more involved when teachers move fairly quickly through coursework and lessons. But a quick pace involves more than just more quickly saying what you usually say. Perhaps the most common mistake in delivering a quick-paced lesson is to keep explaining ideas to students in slightly different ways. I used to do this. I explained something, realized I could say it another way, and explained it again. Then I asked, "Any questions?" By now, the students who had understood what I said the first time had begun to get restless. Sometimes a student said he did have a question. Then I was stuck. Could I refuse his request for assistance? Usually not. Most often I explained the topic a third time, making it difficult for the students who already understood to stay alert.

When you already understand something, listening to repeated explanations of it is like waiting in a slow line—in a word, frustrating. Nothing dampens the learning energy of students more than waiting around for something that interests them, something they can dig their mental teeth into. I have learned over the years to avoid asking "Any questions?" When I sometimes slip and do ask that question, I usually follow it with this question: "How many others have questions and would like us to come back to this another time?" Or I might say: "I'll bet more of you have that same question. Pair up with someone nearby and talk over your understanding with each other, helping those who still have questions." Either of these responses is less likely to slow the pace of a lesson than a repeated explanation is. More fundamentally, I'm always searching for teaching strategies that give me alternative ways of helping students who have questions. I've included in this book some strategies I've found effective: Learning Pairs, Ask a Friend, Sharing Pairs, Review Test, Support Group, Class Tutors, and "I Say" Review.

The pace of choice, especially with restless students, is the quick pace, the pace of high involvement, the pace that keeps consciousness high. It usually translates into lessons composed of many short steps, each involving a change in either topic or procedure. I recommend you make the change as soon as you sense student involvement is diminishing, as when energy seems to wane or attention drifts from the subject. The change is usually best done sooner, not later. Once students become disengaged, you'll need to make an extra effort to get them fully involved.

For slower students, use the power of expectations: that is, expect them to speed up to your pace; do not slow to theirs. Step ahead at a pace that energizes student awareness and keeps as many students as possible actively involved in the lesson. Remember, however, to plan to return to selected topics again and again so students know they will have another opportunity to "get it" later if they do not understand now. Strategies for planning the revisiting of topics are included in Chapters 2 and 12.

Should you ever slow the pace? In some cases, yes. For those of you whose minds tend to snap along too fast, slowing down may be the wise adjustment, especially when topics require more than the usual thinking. You might then pause longer, speak more deliberately. Or you might ask students to do some reflecting and note taking or to exchange thoughts with a partner. You also might want to slow down when students get too frazzled and need to be calmed. You must, of course, learn to adjust the pace of instruction so that it is appropriate for your students and for the topic being studied. I believe most teachers are more likely to belabor a point than rush through it. We also are likely to re-explain a point rather than let it go for another day. So for most of us, most of the time, the speed of choice should be the quick pace.

A Teacher Comments

After you talked about quick pace, I became very aware when the pace was too slow for some students. My biggest example was board work. I had some students putting work on the board while others in the room sat in dead time, just watching. Worse yet, I would ask the board writers to explain their work, which often produced more dead time in audience eyes. I discontinued doing that. When I have board work now, I have all students doing desk work at the same time. And when I need something explained, I do it myself and keep the pace moving.
—Vicki Summers, mathematics teacher

Strategy 1.3: Teaching in Layers, Not Lumps

Description: Returning to topics from time to time, rather than aiming for mastery at any one time, so learnings are reinforced over time and the risk of losing student involvement is minimized.

Purpose: To take the pressure for instant learning off students and to allow them to learn at a more personally natural pace.

Focusing on one topic for a long period of time isn't necessarily the best way to help students achieve mastery. I've found that returning briefly but frequently to a topic often better helps students learn it fully and deeply. We can overlap content and spiral ahead to mastery. We can teach in layers, not lumps. For example, as shown in Lesson Plan 2 on pages 15 and 16, students can handle previously presented material by participating in choral work, by engaging in guided practice, by hearing the teacher think aloud, and by completing a review test. Teaching in layers helps students learn content in much the same way people learn their native language: by dealing with it again and again, allowing mastery to develop gradually.

If you use this strategy, plan lessons that keep touching on prior material until students have achieved sufficient mastery. This book includes many teaching strategies to help you teach in layers.

Strategy 1.4: Limited Variety ─────────────

Description: Variety in a classroom sufficient to keep students involved, yet no so diverse as to threaten students' security and need for predictability.

Purpose: To prevent lesson variety from becoming too confusing and unsettling for students.

Too much variety can raise student anxiety. Most students—and teachers—need a certain level of routine to feel secure. This strategy involves finding the level that allows you and your students to work well together. This level will likely change as you and your students become more accustomed to one another.

Don't let students' initial unfamiliarity with your teaching strategies throw you off your general approach to high-involvement lessons. Remember that the first few times you use a new teaching strategy, students may appear anxious because they're not quite sure what you're doing. Eventually they will become familiar and comfortable with the teaching strategies and quickly move from one activity to another. You can help students feel secure enough to handle the variety of teaching strategies you use by establishing and maintaining some general routines. For instance, you may always begin class in the same way or handle homework in the same way. Change topics often, but within familiar structures. Change lesson sequences, but without abandoning familiar elements. You can use a large variety of strategies if you keep using and re-using them, so students feel comfortable with them.

* * *

Now that we've looked at the four strategies for planning high-involvement lessons, let's turn to additional strategies that might help you carry out these four strategies. As you read ahead, you may want to return occasionally to this chapter to consider just how you might use a certain strategy to achieve a high-involvement lesson.

2 Basic Instructional Strategies

The focus of Chapter 1 was on planning whole-class lessons that draw students into active involvement and keep them involved. This chapter discusses teaching strategies that are particularly useful in conducting such lessons. Although some of these strategies may be familiar to you, this chapter will probably give you some new ideas for using them. I look at the strategies as a basic tool kit for conducting high-involvement lessons. Note that all the strategies discussed in this chapter were mentioned in Chapter 1.

Strategy 2.1: Whip Around, Pass Option

Description: Asking each student in turn to speak to an issue or to say "I pass."

Purpose: To increase the number of students who speak up and to give students practice in responsible self-management.

Sometimes we want to hear from many students, not just a few volunteers. In such situations, try saying: "Let's whip down the row of students by the window. When it comes your turn, either give your thoughts or say 'I pass.' You don't have to respond if you prefer not to. Let's go!"

The Whip Around, Pass Option strategy can be used with all or part of a class. It is especially useful when the question asked will likely draw a variety of responses. It provides an efficient way of getting students to share their different perspectives. Here are two more examples of how to use this strategy:

• "We all have different ideas on _____. Let's start with Bob and whip around the whole class, giving each person a chance to share one idea. You can always say 'I pass.' But first take a moment to think about what idea you might want to share. [Pause.] Okay, Bob, please start us off."

• "Look over the outcome sentences you wrote about that chapter. I'd like to whip around at least part of the class now and ask you to read just one of your sentences. If you'd rather not read yours, say 'I pass.' Let's start today with Helen." (See Strategy 2.3 on page 25 for a discussion of outcome sentences.)

The Whip Around, Pass Option strategy not only gives all students a chance to voice their ideas, it raises the interest level of a class. Students often listen closely to how others respond to an issue to which they also have a response. The strategy also works well with shy students who may not otherwise offer answers in class. In addition, it poses a valuable self-management choice to all students: Should I risk speaking up or risk passing? For some students in some situations, saying "I pass" might be the greater risk. In any case, offering students a choice invites them to practice managing their lives wisely and responsibly.

A Teacher Comments

I discovered that the Whip Around, Pass Option strategy makes students more responsible. I've used it quite a lot and have noticed lately that the students who passed because that was the "cool" thing to do are now participating. It has been really great to see the progression of these boys from everyone wanting to pass to 99 percent participation. It took a while, but the wait was worth it.

—Linda Prater

Strategy 2.2: Question, All Write

Description: Students each writing an answer to a question before the teacher calls on one student or announces the correct answer.

Purpose: To maximize the number of students who think about a question.

When posing questions to a group of students, it is useful to pause between asking a question and calling on someone to respond. That pause or "wait time," as Mary Budd Rowe (1974) calls it, is designed to give all students a chance to frame an answer in their mind. Without wait time, many students are likely to sit passively, waiting for the students who are always ready to give the answer.

Two major problems are common with wait time. First, teachers often find it difficult to pause after every question. A teacher's instinct is usually to keep the class busy, and wait time can feel like an invitation to restlessness. Second, many students fail to use wait time to frame their answers precisely. The Question, All Write strategy helps overcome these problems. Asking students to quickly scribble an answer provides the necessary pause for thinking, and the writing pushes students to think more precisely about the question.

Once a fair number of students have written their answers, a teacher might ask, "How many would be willing to read something they wrote?" Since all students have had a chance not only to think but to write, and since they need not improvise an answer orally but can simply read what they wrote, more students are usually ready to speak up. Moreover, if the question has only one correct response, then all students have their own private response before them to compare with the correct answer. All students, therefore, have a better opportunity for active learning.

Some teachers ask a question and have students write an answer on a small personal chalkboard or slate and then hold up the slate when they've finished. One advantage to this variation is that you can tell from the easily visible answers how well the class understands the question. You can also personally acknowledge students who have the correct answer and quickly spot students who are working carelessly or not working at all.

There are important disadvantages to this variation as well: Slow students are often embarrassed at having to show imperfect work. Furthermore, the emphasis of the strategy shifts from activating students' thinking to obtaining answers that are checked by the teacher, an approach far less inspirational. The original strategy motivates more students to do their best thinking.

Strategy 2.3: Outcome Sentences

Description: Sentences students write after reflecting on a lesson or experience, prompted by such phrases as *I learned . . . , I'm beginning to wonder . . . , I was surprised . . .*

Purpose: To help students create meaningful learnings for themselves and to help them develop the habit of learning from experience.

We want students' learning to be *meaningful* to them, to make sense to them, not be merely strings of words they are forced to remember. Moreover, we want students to be *lifelong* learners, to learn how to learn on their own, to learn how to gain meaning from experience after they leave school. The Outcome Sentences strategy is designed to serve these purposes. It can be built on almost any classroom experience. For instance, let's say a social studies teacher takes 30 minutes to tell anecdotes about an event in history, show a map of the region involved, and explain what he thinks about the event. The teacher might then say, "Please reflect on the discussion and see if you can find some learnings for yourself from it. Look at this chart. It contains phrases you might want to complete as you explore what you learned. You might, for example, begin just by writing 'I learned . . . ' Or you might start a sentence with the phrase 'I was surprised . . . ' or 'I'm beginning to wonder . . . ' or any similar phrase that comes to mind. Think back over our discussion and write your thoughts about it."

After students have taken a few minutes to write their thoughts, the teacher might proceed in one of two ways:

• He asks whether anyone is willing to read one of their outcome sentences. The class listens to a few volunteers. Then the teacher asks students to pair up and share some of their "I learned" statements with each other. The two sharing processes help students see ideas in the lesson that they had not noticed.

• He starts a whip-around, giving each student a turn either to read one outcome sentence to the whole class or to say "I pass."

Either option can lead into a whole-class summary discussion, with the teacher adding the points he wants to emphasize.

Tips for Using the Outcome Sentences Strategy

• Use the Outcome Sentences strategy by asking students to write outcome sentences for each chapter they read in a textbook; each group project they complete; presentations by guest speakers; discussions of current events, films, units completed; their holiday vacations; the first week of school; the stories they read; each day's class.

• Keep an "I Learned" chart posted, so students have handy thinking starters whenever they are asked to review what they learned.

• Periodically add other phrases to the chart, such as: I now realize that . . . , I would someday like to . . . , I would conclude . . . . , I cannot agree with . . . , I would like to find out more about . . .

• Ask students to keep their outcome sentences in a Learning Log, or use them as material for a student portfolio, which could later be used to summarize and illustrate each student's accomplishments.

• Do not expect all students to get the *same* learning from a lesson. The aim of this strategy is to help students digest information and create personal meaning for themselves.

A Teacher Comments

I used the Outcome Sentences strategy to wrap up our weather unit. After reviewing our unit, we charted as a group all our learnings. Then each child picked one that they liked and wrote it on a raindrop pattern. The raindrops were placed on our April bulletin board.

—Susan Willis

Strategy 2.4: Underexplain with Learning Pairs

Description: Explaining material briefly, so that only some students fully understand it, and then asking pairs to work together to help each other learn the material.

Purpose: To keep students actively involved in learning, exercise students' thinking power, and encourage students to develop the ability to support one another in the classroom.

Imagine the following mathematics lesson:

A teacher says to her class: "To find 40% of a number, we simply multiply the number by .40. For example, 40% of 200 is done like this:

$$
\begin{array}{r}
200 \\
\times\ .40 \\
\hline
000 \\
800 \\
\hline
80.00
\end{array}
$$

Try a problem like this one by yourself. Let's see what you think 40% of 120 is."

The students work alone at their desks, trying to solve the problem.

"How many of you got 48 as your answer?" Most of the students raise their hands in response.

"While you were working the problem at your desk, I worked it here on the board. How many did it pretty much like I did it?" Several students raise their hands. "How many found another way to get 48?"

The teacher asks a few of the students who raise their hand what they did differently, but she avoids having a long discussion here. She keeps the pace moving.

"I've put three more problems on the board. First work them by yourself. Then turn to a partner. Compare answers and help each other understand how you got your answers. If both of you understand, try creating a new problem for each other, maybe a harder one. Go!"

Once students start their work, the teacher begins working the problems correctly on board, so all can look to the board for help if they need it. She walks around the room, scanning students' work and answering most questions with, "Ask another pair of students for help."

When about half the pairs seem to have finished, she calls out, "Just a few more seconds." She doesn't wait for all students to finish, but makes a mental note of what needs reteaching and review.

Once students have broken out of their pairs, the teacher says, "It looks like most of you worked the problems pretty much the way I did on the board. Here are three more problems that are just a bit harder," she says, as she writes three more problems on the board. "Again, work these problems alone and then compare your answers and how you got your answers with your partner. If both of you understand the calculations, challenge each other with something more difficult. Or write out a word problem that I can someday use in class and put it on my desk. Go!"

The teacher in this example *underexplained* the calculation procedure. Many teachers do the opposite; they overexplain. For instance, they explain, ask if anyone has questions, and then explain again. Or they notice some obviously puzzled students and explain again for their benefit. Or they explain in different words just to make sure everyone gets it. After two or three such explanations, three results are likely:

1. Students who understood the first explanation—or who understood the subject before the lesson even began—become bored. They tune out and their energy level drops.

2. Students who cannot concentrate their awareness on one topic for very long become bored. Like the students above, they tune out and their energy level drops.

3. Students who need to discover things for themselves, often from practical experience, tune out. Their energy level drops too.

The Underexplain with Learning Pairs strategy can help you avoid such outcomes. Another example of the Underexplain with Learning Pairs strategy can be found in Action Flow Lesson 3 on page 16.

Tips for Using the Underexplain with Learning Pairs Strategy

• Explain your subject only until about half the students in the class understand it. Then put students into pairs to teach each other, check each other's understanding, or create new problems for each other.

• Leave students in pairs for only a short time, so that confused students don't feel lost and other students don't get bored by their inaction. The time to move ahead is when you sense students will soon move off task. When in doubt, move rather more quickly than slowly. If the subject matter is suitable, you might bring students back into pairs to do some additional work after a whole-group discussion, perhaps slightly raising the level of challenge.

• Don't prod students who are slow to get to work. Pressuring students is usually counterproductive in the long run. Instead, move the lesson along quickly, giving enough easy examples so students eventually and naturally want to be involved.

• In most cases, allow students to form their own pairs. Choosing partners can be a useful challenge to students' developing responsibility. You may choose to help find partners for students who don't find partners on their own, or you may choose to leave them alone or talk to them later and encourage them to risk reaching out to others more often, to practice taking the initiative in such situations. Consider what would be best for each student in the long run. This issue and other common problems of group work are discussed further in Chapter 8.

One strength of the Underexplain with Learning Pairs strategy flows from the expectations it communicates. The more often this strategy is used, the more students are likely to appreciate the fact that a responsible adult, the teacher, fully expects them to be able to think and learn and to support and help one another. Even if students never need to use the skills or ideas learned during this activity or one day forget the details, they will come to believe that each of them is an able person.

You may recognize that the Underexplain with Learning Pairs strategy is similar to Arthur Whimbey's paired problem solving (Whimbey and Lochhead 1986). You may also want to explore the literature on inductive teaching as, for example, discussed by Jerome Bruner (Bruner and Kenny 1966).

A Teacher Comments

*I tried using the Underexplain with Learning Pairs strategy to intro-
duce a program in computers. It worked great! Those who knew a lot
about computers just took right off. Those who didn't really caught on
from their peers.*

—Cheryl Miller

Strategy 2.5: Voting

Description: Asking questions to which students can respond nonverbally, as by asking, "How many of you . . . ?"

Purpose: To sample student thinking without slowing the pace of a lesson.

Questions requiring verbal responses obviously slow the pace of a lesson, sometimes unnecessarily. When our intent in asking a question is to appraise the class's understanding, we need not beat around the bush. We can save time and keep the lesson moving by using what I call voting questions—that is, questions students can answer simply by raising their hands. As you can see from the list of questions below, it's easy to turn verbal-response questions into voting questions:

Verbal-response questions	*Voting questions*
1. Does anyone have any questions?	1. How many have questions they would still like to clear up?
2. Are we ready to move on?	2. How many are ready to move on?

3. Do you agree with what Ginger just said?

3. How many agree with Ginger? How many disagree?

Voting questions keep student involvement high because (1) they allow us to avoid student comments that can slow class progress and (2) they make it easy for all students to participate in the questions raised, so all feel involved.

You may also consider asking students to use one of these more complex nonverbal responses:

• *Degrees of agreement.* "If you agree, raise your hand all the way. If you half agree, raise it halfway. If you disagree, point thumbs down."

• *Readiness to respond.* "Hold up one finger if you have an idea but do not want me to call on you, just so I know who has an idea. Hold up two fingers if you are willing to respond aloud but are really not all that sure. Hold up three fingers if you are fairly sure and are willing to respond. Otherwise hold up a fist, so I'll know how many really have no idea. I'll call on only those holding up two or three fingers."

A Teacher Comments

We used the "Voting" strategy several times last week. One example was in a science lesson. We were discussing properties of matter, specifically, sinking or floating. Each child tested one object by placing it in a tub of water. Before doing so, the class voted on whether the object would sink or float. This kept everyone involved and interested in the activity, which was rather lengthy. Second graders love to vote on anything!

—Ginny Beatty

Strategy 2.6: Ask a Friend

Description: A recommendation that students needing help "ask a friend."

Purpose: To nurture a feeling of mutual support among students and save teacher time and energy.

My first response to a student who asks what page we are on, or who asks me to repeat the homework directions, or who is unsure of how to complete a worksheet is usually "Please ask a friend." This statement serves me in several ways. It eases my load, because most students have little difficulty getting the help they need from other students. It generates mutual respect and appreciation among students and builds a healthy, interdependent class community. It communicates that others in the class can be "friends" if only we see them as such.

Grace Pilon (1991), from whom I learned this strategy, notes that some elementary students invent confusions in order to ask the teacher for help. For such students, asking one friend may not be enough. Moorman and Moorman (1989) offer the phrase "Ask three then me." For instance, they might tell students, "Whenever you are working at individual tasks and need assistance, please ask three other people in the classroom for help before asking me." When a student approaches afterward, a teacher might then remind the student, "Please ask three then me." Or simply inquire, "Did you ask three before me?"

A Teacher Comments

At first, some of the children found asking a friend difficult because they wanted an immediate answer from the teacher—they weren't sure they could trust all their peers for the correct answer. After the third time of Ask a Friend, the students became more trusting of each other.
—Miriam Harmon

Strategy 2.7: Sharing Pairs

Description: Students pairing up and sharing thoughts.

Purpose: To give students practice in talking about their ideas and listening to others.

Asking students to talk about ideas is a great way to get them actively involved in a learning task. The most activity comes when they talk in pairs because each person is then either a talker or a listener; no one is left out (see Chapter 8 for more on group size and selection).

The Sharing Pairs strategy not only invites active involvement, it also compels students to put into words ideas that may still be a bit unclear in their minds. This strategy also meets students' basic needs for social contact and freedom of expression.

Sharing can be used frequently and in many situations:

• **To share opinions.** For instance, say to the class, "Many people disagree about _____. Before we discuss this as a group, please pair up and exchange your thoughts or questions with one person. We'll take just a few minutes for this sharing." Students then form pairs and share thoughts.

• **To exchange understandings.** Ask students to form pairs and share their outcome sentences from the day's lesson or from homework.

• **During a lecture.** To give students a chance to put ideas into their own words and thereby get more meaning from a lecture, ask them to "take a few moments and share your reactions to what I've said so far with someone nearby."

• **After the Question, All Write strategy.** On a question with multiple answers: "Please share your thoughts with a partner and then we'll get together and see what we all think."

• **In the midst of a discussion.** To give many students who have something to say the chance to voice their ideas or confusions.

• **To add energy to the room.** When most students have been working alone for a while or have been mainly listening to others, ask them to "take a few minutes and share your thoughts or your work with one other person."

A Teacher Comments

I tried Sharing Pairs when working with prepositional phrases in my slower English classes. We had been working with prepositions for a few days, and homework was going slowly. Instead of having students take work home, I asked them to choose a partner and do sentences together. Students were pleasantly surprised at the progress they made when they helped each other. This was a very productive class for everyone.

—*Cathy McGarrahan*

Strategy 2.8: Choral Work

Description: Students repeating information aloud in unison, often responding to flash cards or teacher prompts.

Purpose: To help students memorize material in a relatively easy way. Also, to heighten student involvement and group energy.

Teachers of young children often have the entire class chant the ABCs. This choral work strategy is valuable at all grade levels and for all kinds of content. The method is basically the same, no matter what the grade level:

1. Collect information you want students to internalize, such as chemical symbols (sodium fluoride = NaF) or proper language phrases (to whom she did speak, he and I went). Print one item on a card and make a stack of cards. Use no more than 10 or 12 cards the first day.

2. Hold up each card and ask students to read aloud what's written on the card. Read each card aloud yourself, moving through the pack briskly and asking students to speak out along with you. Keep moving. Expect students to come along with you.

3. Tell students you will use choral work like this for a few minutes from time to time, so they can easily place material deep in their memories.

4. On subsequent days, as the material on the flash cards becomes familiar to students, you can add new cards. If the stack gets too large, eliminate old cards. From time to time, however, reintroduce old cards to reactivate and deepen prior knowledge.

The first time you use this strategy, students will notice your confidence and, soon enough, most will be chanting the cards in a choral style. After several days, almost all students will participate.

You can make stacks of cards for any content you want students to internalize: states and their capitals, multiplication facts ($7 \times 5 = 35$), tricky spelling words, formulas (area of triangle = $1/2bh$), important health principles (fruits and vegetables provide many essential vitamins). Some teachers use cards like these every day to pep up their class. Choral work brings the voices in a room together, contributing to the development of a community of learners. It can also be a valuable change of pace. And, little by little, as students internalize the material on the cards, they come to enjoy the confidence of calling out correct answers again and again.

Here are some tips for using the Choral Work strategy:

• **Keep the cards turning.** Do not worry that some students do not know the information on a card or say it incorrectly. Do not bother to correct students. Repeating cards will help students internalize the correct information. And do not worry that some students already know the information. If the pace is quick, they will enjoy being part of the group, using their voices, and expressing their knowledge.

• **The back of card can be for you.** By writing the same information on the back and front of the card, you can easily show students the information and see it yourself. After a bit, most teachers find they do not need to see the information or chant along with students. Students chant with enthusiasm by themselves.

• **Insert a pause for thought.** Choral work is particularly effective for memorizing facts that come in pairs: a state and its capital, a chemical name and its symbol, basic multiplication facts. You may want to put one element of the pair on the front of the card and the other on the back. For instance, let's say you're using multiplication flash cards. You say to the class, "Here are cards with multiplication facts. I'll show the problem on the card, like this one, $4 \times 5 =$___. Then we'll chant the problem together. Then we'll have a beat of silence, so you can think of the answer. Finally, I'll flip over the card like this to show the answer— 20. And then together we'll chant the answer. Let's try it."

Incidentally, some teachers are tempted to show only the "question" part of the card, such as $7 \times 6 =$___. They do not want to give students the answers. I do not recommend that practice. The process of showing the question, allowing a beat for students to think, and then showing the answer better meets the aim of helping students deeply internalize information because it enables them to concentrate on the information without worrying about being right or wrong.

• **Periodically encourage students to increase the group's energy.** An important benefit of choral work is in the group energy it generates. To reach peak energy levels, however, the group sometimes needs some help from the teacher in the form of encouragement. For example, "Say it with power," or "Speak up as if you mean it," or "A little more energy please," or "With more gusto."

• **Distinguish between energy and loudness.** When the noise level in the classroom needs to be modulated, demonstrate the difference between a soft, energetic voice and a weak, thin voice. Show that people can even whisper with high energy. Then request voices that are powerful without being loud. Students learn they can speak clearly and firmly without being too loud.

• **Use sound variety.** For variety, ask students to speak more or less loudly depending on how high the cards are being held. Cards held at shoulder height, for example, signal that students should speak with a healthy volume. Cards held waist high, on the other hand, signal students to speak strongly but in a whisper.

• **One say, all say.** Pilon (1987a) recommends we sometimes ask all students to respond in unison after one student has read a card aloud. The procedure works this way: Hold up a card. Students willing to read it aloud raise hands; you nod at one. That student reads the card aloud, and then you say "Everyone," and the entire class repeats what that student said. I occasionally use a similar procedure in other lesson formats:

Teacher:	What is the definition of a noun?
Jacob:	A person, place, or thing.
Teacher:	Yes, a noun is a person, place, or thing. All together, class . . .
Entire Class:	A noun is a person, place, or thing.

• **Use One Say, All Say for emphasis.** The One Say, All Say option can be used to reinforce any special content. For instance:

Teacher:	It is important to see the environment as one whole system. Together, please say that with me.
Entire Class:	The environment is one whole system.
Teacher:	Let's say it again, with more power.
Entire Class:	The environment is one whole system.

Teacher: Yes, it is important to see that the environment is one whole, interdependent, active system that . . .

A Teacher Comments

I tried Choral Work with my Essentials of Algebra/Geometry class. We were studying the names of the polygons. I would say, "A ten-sided polygon is called _____." The class would say, "Decagon." I went through all of them from three sides to ten sides, twelve and fifteen sides slowly. Then we went faster and faster through all the polygons. This was a great way for the students to memorize the polygons and to participate as a whole class.

—Cindy Huels

Strategy 2.9: Attentive Lecture

Description: A lecture ended before student attention begins to slip.

Purpose: To keep all students attentive in lectures.

If given the opportunity, some educators would eliminate lectures because they believe lectures reduce learning to a passive process. I disagree. I have known teachers whose lectures keep students actively involved for a long time. Most of us, unfortunately, don't have that level of skill. But we can lecture well enough for short periods. And we will likely find situations in which a short lecture is the appropriate form of instruction.

The key to the Attentive Lecture strategy is to keep an eye out for the first signs that students' attention is drifting and to stop that drift before awareness falls too far. Pulling students back is not easy, but it can be done by, in effect, shifting gears. How does one make these shifts? There is no single formula, but here are examples of two transitions I often use:

• **The write-share shift.** If the lecture is rich in content worth thinking about, I often use a two-step shift. First, I ask students to make notes on what they've heard so far: "Perhaps write the main points, or your questions, or your personal reactions." When I see that one or two students have finished making notes, I say, "One moment more."

Second, I ask all students to sit with a partner and share thoughts. While they do this, I consider what might best follow these sharing pairs. A discussion is often appropriate. Sometimes I can even resume my lecture. But sometimes I find it best to put the issue aside and come back fresh another time.

• **The quick review and out.** Sometimes the content is routine or is essentially factual. It is usually inappropriate to ask students to reflect on this kind of content and write their thoughts, as in the shift above. I might then quickly review what I covered and tell students we will pick up the material another time. Or I might ask a few students to restate a point they remember. Or I might simply say: "Before we turn to something new, please take a moment and review for yourself what we covered, perhaps noting questions you have." The quick pace is important here. I do not want to let students' attention drift any further away, so I leave the lecture quickly.

Strategy 2.10: Speak-Write

Description: A lecture procedure containing occasional pauses that students know are for writing personal reactions, a summary of what they heard, questions, or anything else they choose.

Purpose: To increase the learning power of lectures.

The Speak-Write strategy is similar to the Attentive Lecture strategy in that it involves shifting from a lecture to another activity. With the Speak-Write strategy, however, the teacher structures beforehand the time for thinking during lectures. Here is an example of a teacher introducing this strategy to a class:

> "I'm going to talk to you about our topic for a little while now. To make sure everyone understands, I'm going to use what's called a Speak-Write procedure. That is, I will speak until I reach a convenient break in the material, but not so long that you need to take notes while I'm talking. I would like you to listen without being distracted by note taking and without being overwhelmed by too much material. So I will speak for perhaps three or four minutes.
> "Then I will pause for a minute or so. When I pause, your job is to write. What do you write? You have four choices. You may

want to write a summary of what you heard me say." The teacher writes "1 - SUMMARY" on the chalkboard. "Or you may want to write questions about what I said." She writes "2 - QUESTIONS" on the board. "Or you may want to write your reactions to what I spoke about. She adds "3 - REACTIONS" to the list. "Or you may write anything else you choose, or draw something if you prefer. Use the time to gather your thoughts in any way that works well for you." She adds "4 - ANYTHING ELSE" to the list.

When I use this strategy, I begin promptly, letting the practice of it show how I intend it to work. I do not invite questions about what I just said, which is likely to lead to repeating my instructions and boring some students. In other words, I strive for a quick pace and move right into my lecture, speaking for a few minutes, pausing for a minute or so for students to make notes, again speaking, then pausing for writing, and so on. In classes in which I lecture often, I leave a small chart posted that reminds students of the four speak-write options outlined in the example above.

Often I follow several speak-write cycles with Sharing Pairs (Strategy 2.7): "Now sit with a partner and compare thoughts and help each other clear up any confusions." This follow-up strategy further helps students digest my lecture material. I often follow Sharing Pairs with a whole-class discussion.

I once thought that if students were older and more mature, I could speak longer than three or four minutes before stopping for writing time, but I have found that during long lectures, students at all grade levels, from kindergarten to college, begin to experience content overload and difficulty maintaining attention.

Incidentally, when using this strategy with young children who cannot write or who have difficulty writing, I usually say: "When I pause, you may write or draw something, if you like, or just sit quietly and see what goes on in your mind as you think back over what I said. Think it over for yourself."

Some people recommend augmenting lectures with lots of visuals, such as overhead projector notes, chalkboard notes, handouts (especially handouts with outlines), sometimes outlines with spaces in which students make notes as the lecture proceeds. All of these are valuable. They give students visual and oral information. They are especially valuable for the many students who learn more from seeing than from hearing. Yet they do not remedy the problem of "too-muchness," which is often the main drawback of lectures. By themselves, visual aids do not give students the time they need to think and thereby construct personal meaning from lectures. I recommend using plenty of visuals, including role playing and demonstrations if appropriate, but also allowing plenty of thinking time, as by inserting silent pauses, using the Speak-Write strategy, or keeping a lecture brief and following it with the two-step shift outlined above.

Strategy 2.11: Attentive Discussion

Description: A class discussion ended before student attention begins to slip.

Purpose: To keep all students involved in discussions.

Teachers often engage a whole class in discussion, but too often only part of the class remains involved. The big talkers talk and the others wait for the time to pass. That leads to the first rule for effective class discussions: Continue class discussions only as long as students remain attentive. Switch strategies as soon as group awareness begins slipping. Considering the attention span of today's students, that moment may come quickly, for it is the rare topic that holds students' attention for longer than a few minutes. Sometimes, however, a discussion can be revitalized by switching to another activity. Let's look at some examples:

• The teacher notices the discussion is dragging, so she decides to use the Voting strategy to shift its course. After one student has finished speaking, she asks, "How many of you agree with what Todd has said? How many disagree? Are unsure?" She then says, "How many people have something else to say? Let's hear from four people now. Okay. Tom and then Jane, and then Sue, and then Rick." Setting up a sequence of speakers relaxes many students and makes them more attentive because they don't have to wonder who will speak next or if they should volunteer to speak (see Strategy 9.2 on p. 121).

• The teacher stops the discussion by using the Question, All Write strategy: "Please take a moment to write down or draw your ideas about what we have been talking about. What do you think about this subject now?" Then she leads into the Sharing Pairs strategy: "Now turn to a neighbor and take two or three minutes to share your thoughts."

• The teacher decides to use the Whip Around, Pass Option strategy to shift the discussion. She says, "Let's use a class whip around. We'll start in this corner. When it's your turn, please tell us your ideas, even if it feels risky to you. In this class, we accept all thinking. Or, if you like, say whose thoughts you agree with. Of course, you may always pass if you'd rather not say anything this time around."

• The teacher uses the Outcome Sentences strategy to shift the discussion: "Before we go on to something else, think back over the discussion and see if you can find some learnings for yourself from it. Let's sample a few and then decide if we want to talk more about this."

The second rule for effective class discussions is equally straightforward: Do not assume discussions always stimulate meaningful thinking. Often discussions only stimulate the exchange of opinions and thoughtless chatter. Discussions usually work best as only part of a more rounded lesson, as in this sequence:

1. Students think about a topic and make notes of preliminary ideas.
2. Students pair up and briefly exchange thoughts.
3. A whole-class discussion takes place, with volunteers speaking.
4. All students think back over the lesson and write outcome sentences, which might then be shared in a class Whip Around, discussed in Sharing Pairs, or placed in portfolios.

Discussions rarely produce as much learning as their high reputation suggests. Most students seem to experience a discussion much like they do a lecture: as a set of statements that do not add up to personal meaning, at least not until the statements are mulled over and digested. And since the statements in a discussion are often disconnected and sometimes repetitious, they are often difficult to mull over and digest. It's best to have short, focused discussions and be ready to shift to other activities when the discussion begins to bog down. To that end, here are some additional ideas for maintaining attentive discussions:

1. Create a provocative topic list. Consider making notes of discussion topics that have worked well for you, and keep your list handy for classroom reference.

2. Appoint a student discussion leader. Perhaps ask a student to lead some discussions and to announce when he or she thinks the class should shift to another activity.

3. Create visuals. Write key words, ideas, and numbers on the chalkboard during a discussion to help students maintain their focus. Some students see better than they hear, and most students benefit when more than one of their senses are actively involved.

4. Appoint chalkboard writers. Ask a student to make notes on the board of key points. This is especially useful when the class is generating a list of ideas. To avoid downtime, use two chalkboard writers so that the second writer can begin a new note while the first is finishing the previous one. When students make rambling comments, it is useful for the teacher to suggest to the writers what phrase to write on the board.

5. Maximize eye contact. Students on the edges of a group or in the back of a room often feel they remain unnoticed. Scan the group, walk around the room, or occasionally change seating to minimize this problem.

6. Move to circle seating. Consider arranging desks in a circle or semicircle for class discussions so all students are close to the center of action. Students who are facing one another, looking one another in the eye as they speak, are more apt to stay involved.

7. Give nods of recognition. To involve students other than the usual big talkers in discussions, perhaps announce that you'll be using nods of recognition instead of calling on the first student to raise a hand. See Strategy 9.3 on page 122 for more information on this practice.

Strategy 2.12: Think Aloud

Description: Talking aloud while working through a problem.

Purpose: To give students a model of how thinking often proceeds. Also, to illustrate that thinking is not always linear.

Students often misunderstand what is involved in thinking through a problem. Many assume that answers come quickly, easily, and without errors—as answers seem to come to the fastest of learners. When that does not happen for them, many lose confidence in their ability to think.

They become learners who must be spoon-fed, able only to memorize, not to think.

We can teach students the truth about problem solving: that it is usually slow and messy and rarely quick and easy. Perhaps the best way to teach this is to model it. Here is an example of a teacher thinking aloud as she works a problem on the chalkboard:

> "Let's see here, I could divide 6 into the 50. Wait a minute. Would that help me find my answer? What was the problem again? Find 1/6 of 50. Dividing feels right. Let me try that and see if I get something that at least looks just about right. If this doesn't work, I'll try to solve it another way.
>
> "Now, let's see, 6 goes into 50 . . . hmmm . . . 6 times 5 is 30, 6 times 7 is, umm, 42. That will fit. 6 times 8 is . . . is . . . 48, which is more like it. 6 times 9 is bound to be too much because 48 is just 2 less than 50. So I'll write 8 here, 4 here and . . . "

With the Think Aloud strategy, you talk in ways that reflect real searching, errors, correction of errors, and other steps that go through the mind of someone who is thinking. The Think Aloud strategy is particularly effective for reassuring students who are reluctant to admit they are confused. It is also effective in promoting real-life problem-solving skills. Consider this teacher, who has just said he will show one way to handle a communication problem:

> "Now how am I going to argue with him when I'm really scared? I'm not sure what will happen. I want to tell him how I feel but . . . I don't know . . . It feels terribly scary. Think I'll make some notes. That might help me keep my mind on this issue.
>
> "To start, what is my purpose? My main purpose is to . . . "
> He continues writing.
>
> "Alternatives . . . Have I thought of all my alternatives? I already wrote down three," he says, pointing to the board, where he had written out the three. "There are probably ideas I haven't thought about. Maybe I'll ask Jean if she has some ideas.
>
> "Now I have notes, but how can I decide? I'd rather forget the whole thing. But I remember my purpose is . . . "

A Teacher Comments

To show my special ed students how to read a new word, I use the Think Aloud strategy like this: "I know the story is about birds. And this

word begins with an R. Maybe it's a kind of bird. Could it be a robin?"
I find that with prodding my special ed students can think that way.
Perhaps it is just that they cannot figure out how to think that way.
After I show them how, they do just fine.

—Bruce Maskow

Strategy 2.13: Guided Practice

Description: Students practicing a skill with teacher guidance, so students gradually move toward excellence.

Purpose: To involve all students in practicing and mastering subject matter.

Posing questions that little by little lead students from easy or familiar examples to new understandings is an extremely effective teaching strategy that is commonly called Guided Practice (Rosenshine 1979, 1983). The strategy is appropriate for teaching not only subject matter but also thinking skills and responsibility. Let's look at several examples:

• **A language arts example.** Using the Question, All Write strategy, the teacher asks all students to write the plural of "fox," a plural they already know. As soon as students begin writing, the teacher writes "foxes" on the board, so students can see the correct answer soon after they finish writing. Students correct their own work and, if necessary, make changes so their work is correct. The teacher avoids discussion at this point.

The teacher then calls out the next word, another easy word or perhaps one that may be less familiar or that may lead to a new plural-making rule. Students begin to write the plural of that word and, as they do so, the teacher writes the correct plural on the board. "If you didn't get this one, don't worry," she says, "The next one may follow the same rule." Her aim is to reassure students and keep them alert to discovering new understandings.

The teacher continues this process at a brisk pace, avoiding extended discussion. The emphasis is on learning by practicing and observing and thinking. While students are working, the teacher glances about, getting a sense of how well students understand. If understanding is low, the teacher inserts extra explanatory comments as appropriate and strives to make subsequent words easy enough so students do come to understand.

• **A mathematics example.** The teacher poses a problem. All students work at their desks. While they work, the teacher solves the problem correctly on the board. Students then check their work. The teacher poses another problem and again solves the problem correctly on the board so students can check themselves. The teacher avoids extended discussions so students who already understand how to do the problem do not become bored and so she can keep the lesson focused on learning through practice.

The aim of guided practice is for students to practice familiar work and then gradually move on to new work. You may have a previously prepared list of problems that range from easy to very difficult, so examples are readily available to lead students toward understanding. You may even have previously prepared sheets of problems correctly worked out in print large enough for the entire class to see with the aid of an overhead projector. In some cases, students who cannot grasp the correct procedure from your examples might be told they can ask a friend, or raise a hand so that someone who understands will come over and assist them, or ask you privately later. Avoid long explanations. Encourage students to think about the examples. Reassure them by saying that it may take some time and practice for everyone to be able to understand what you're studying. Tell them you'll try to give examples that show them how to handle key points. Tell them, "Take your time and you will get it."

Sometimes, you may decide to shift, temporarily or completely, from this self-checking practice to a strategy that involves more direct instruction, such as the Think Aloud strategy or the Underexplain with Learning Pairs strategy.

The Guided Practice strategy is essentially a method of teaching by discovery, with students led forward in fairly small steps. As long as students see the strategy as one of learning, not one that tests prior learnings, Guided Practice is naturally motivating to students. Such motivation comes from inside students themselves, *not* from your urging them to strive for excellence or from your checking of their work. Indeed, no scores need be tallied, no grades given. Self-checking practice elicits students' natural desire to do well. Lesson Plan 2 on page 15 contains an additional example of the Guided Practice strategy.

Strategy 2.14: Review Test ────────────

Description: The teacher asking a series of questions about prior material, all students writing an answer to each question, and the teacher announcing the correct answer, either orally or in writing, after each question.

Purpose: To involve all students in reviewing subject matter and correcting misunderstandings. Also, to give students success experiences in school work.

───────────────────────────────

The Review Test strategy is similar to the Guided Practice strategy, except that it is designed not so much for teaching as for reviewing and correcting prior learnings. The Review Test covers material previously introduced in class. The "test" is for each student alone: How many review questions can each student correctly answer? The teacher's role is to test class understanding in a general way by scanning the room during the activity and getting a sense of how well students understand. The primary focus, however, is not to assess learning but to have students review and clarify prior content in a way that is interesting and involving to all. Let's look at a few examples:

• **A language arts example.** The teacher asks students to write on scrap paper the correct spelling of "generosity." As students begin to write, the teacher turns to the chalkboard and writes the correct spelling of the word. When students finish writing their version of the word, they look up, check their work and, if necessary, correct their spelling, so each student has the word spelled correctly.

Without much delay, the teacher then says, "Second word. Classic. The book was a classic. Classic." Students begin to write that word. As they write, the teacher spells the word correctly on the board. To avoid having any student inactive for long, the pace is brisk. The teacher expects students to speed up to her pace rather than ask her to slow to theirs. Students check their work. The teacher says the next word. And the process continues for ten spelling words. Without discussion to slow the process, the teacher has students writing each word and checking their own work.

After calling out 10 spelling words, the teacher might use the voting strategy, asking the following questions: How many feel good about their work? How many were able to correct a mistake? How many found one or more words you need to add to your list of spelling practice words? The teacher might then say, "When you get into your learning pairs tomorrow, drill each other on the words you misspelled, plus a few of your old practice words."

• **A mathematics example.** "Problem one," says the teacher, writing on the board:

1. $(a+4)(a+5) =$

Students begin to work the problem. As they lower their heads to write, the teacher works the problem on the board. When students finish their work, they look up and see:

1. $(a+4)(a+5) = a^2 + 4a + 5a + 20 = a^2 + 9a + 20$

Students check their work and make corrections if necessary. The teacher notices that two or three students are confused, so he makes the next problem very similar to the first one, expecting that the model for the first problem, left on the board, will help those who are confused. "Problem two," he says, as he writes:

2. $(b + 6)(b + 3) =$

Again, as students begin to work, the teacher works the problem correctly on the board. And the process continues for several problems, all without much discussion.

Review Tests like these can be given every day. They may include one or two questions from old material to refresh old memories and then move into recent material to deepen understandings and, as students correct their work, clear up misunderstandings.

A Review Test can also be used to bring students' attention to a new topic. Before introducing longitude, for example, a teacher could have a five-question Review Test on latitude. A Review Test is an efficient way to help students practice and clarify learnings. Most students enjoy the strategy because, with each Review Test, they see how much they have learned. And they have the chance to better understand subjects they are still confused about by risking answers and getting the correct responses without feeling threatened in any way.

I use a variety of Review Test questions in my graduate classes for teachers. My first two or three questions are usually factual, such as "What psychologist wrote about a hierarchy of human needs?" When the teachers start writing their answers, I write on the chalkboard: *1. Abraham Maslow.* Without discussion, I move on as soon as students have checked the board. After the class is into the rhythm of the strategy, I ask more complex questions, such as "What are some purposes served by the Outcome Sentences strategy?" I do not write an answer to this question on the board. Instead, I simply wait until teachers make some notes and then ask for volunteers to share one idea. In this way, I intersperse simple right-wrong questions with questions that have many correct answers. Again, the intent is to give participants a chance to review and refresh prior knowledge and, no small matter, feel good about having already learned something, all in a nonthreatening way.

Another example of the Review Test strategy appears in Lesson Plan 2 of the Action Flow Lesson Plan strategy on page 16.

A Teacher Comments

A slight variation of the Review Test strategy I tried is using the Review Test with Sharing Pairs. I have students work with a friend to try to get the solution to the problem before I put the answer on the board. This method is effective because it creates a lot of aliveness and community in the classroom.

—Cindy Huels

3

Strategies for Expanding Student Confidence

Many students suffer anxiety in the classroom. They worry about how to please the teacher, about whether they'll ever understand what is being taught, about how their classmates will react to their mistakes. Some are so afraid of making mistakes that they are unwilling to participate in activities where they might look foolish or show ignorance. In short, they are afraid of learning. What can we do to help students become comfortable in the classroom? How can we help them approach lessons with assurance, confident that they will learn? Here are two strategies created by Pilon (1981b, 1987a, 1991) that many teachers find very effective.

Strategy 3.1: Truth Signs

Description: Posted signs that remind students of important truths about learning and living.

Purpose: To help students become perceptive, balanced, self-responsible learners.

Truth signs are not the typical signs seen in classrooms. They don't tell students what to do (*Respect the rights of others. Raise your hand before speaking.*); nor do they threaten (*one infraction = 10 minutes off free time*). Truth signs simply remind the class of important truths about learning and living, such as "Everyone needs time to think and learn." In this

49

section, you'll see how one teacher introduced this truth sign and several others to a middle-school class.

> The teacher holds up a sign for students to see, reading it aloud: *"Everyone needs time to think and learn.* Now let's read this together," the teacher says.
>
> "Everyone needs time to think and learn," recites the class.
>
> "Let's say it again, with power."
>
> "Everyone needs time to think and learn," says the class, with more intensity.
>
> "It's true, isn't it?" the teacher says. "When we hear something or try something, we don't usually learn it right away. We need some time to make sense of it, to get it inside us. Even if I say something simple, like 'My mother was born in England,' it might take a second for you to make sense of what those words mean.
>
> "I want to post this sign on our wall so we remember it. It's an important truth. And it can help us keep our learning climate healthy. You can use it as a reminder to give yourself enough time when you want to learn something. You don't want to rush the learning process. Why? Because *everyone needs time to think and learn.*
>
> "Let's read the words aloud again, together, to help us internalize this truth, get it more fully inside us. All together: *Everyone needs time to think and learn.*"
>
> The class chants, "Everyone needs time to think and learn."
>
> "Let's look at another sign: *We each learn in our own ways, by our own time clocks.* Let's say it all together."
>
> "We each learn in our own ways, by our own time clocks," says the class.
>
> "And again," the teacher says. "This time with more power."
>
> "We each learn in our own ways, by our own time clocks," repeats the class.
>
> "This sign, too, is true," the teacher says. "We each learn in our own ways, no one quite like the other. Some of us learn best from words, some from pictures, some from experimenting, some from talking things out with other people. We each have our own favorite ways. It's true, isn't it?
>
> "And we each learn according to our own time clocks, some fast, some slow, all of us only when the time is right for us. For instance, I didn't learn to spell very well until I was much older than my classmates. My time for learning to spell just did not come when it came to most of my classmates. But later, when the time was right, I became a fairly good speller. Maybe you've had a similar experience. How many of you have tried to learn

something, or were told you *should* learn something, but just couldn't do it until you were older, until somehow the time became right?"

Several students raise their hands in response.

"It's true that we each learn in our own ways and by our own time clocks. We want to remember this sign. Let's say it again together, to get it deeper inside us."

"We each learn in our own ways, by our own time clocks," the class chants.

"Again, this time with energy," says the teacher.

"We each learn in our own ways, by our own time clocks," says the class.

"We'll keep this sign in our classroom to remind us of this truth. Sometimes we forget it. We may think we *should* learn something the way others are learning it, but their way may not be the best for us. We have to search for our own best ways to learn. Or we may think we should have learned something *already*, because others have already learned it. That kind of thinking may just get us feeling down on ourselves. And that only makes it harder for us to keep up our energy and keep on learning. So, please don't get down on yourself if you don't learn the way other people learn, and if you don't learn *when* other people learn. That would be foolish, for we each learn in our *own* ways, by our *own* time clocks, right?"

"Right!" says the class.

"Here's another sign: *It's okay to make mistakes. That's the way we learn*," reads the teacher. "Let's say that together."

"It's okay to make mistakes. That's the way we learn," repeats the class.

"And again."

"It's okay to make mistakes. That's the way we learn."

"And this statement, too, is true," the teacher says. "Even the first time we walked, we stumbled, fell down, got up, and tried again. The first time we try anything we are apt to make mistakes, so it makes no sense to get down on ourselves when we make those mistakes. If we do that, we can eventually become so afraid of making mistakes that we are afraid to even try anything. And that is silly. It's okay to make mistakes. That's the way we learn. Mistakes just happen when we start learning.

"Now, all together again: *It's okay to make mistakes. That's the way we learn*."

"It's okay to make mistakes. That's the way we learn," the class says.

"We want to remember that making mistakes is not something unfortunate. It's necessary. It's the way we learn," emphasizes the teacher.

"Now look at this sign: *It's intelligent to ask for help. No one need do it all alone.* This is true. If I need to do something I don't know how to do, it's intelligent to ask for help from someone who *does* know how to do it. Then I get what I need and, often, the other person gets the pleasure of helping. Don't you sometimes feel good when you can help someone? That's what people in a community do, help one another. One person delivers the mail. Another mows the lawn. Another cooks. Another builds. Old folks sit outside and smile on us. Young people play outside and act silly. It takes all of us to make a community. No one does it all alone. We help one another.

"It is *intelligent* to help one another. It would be dumb for someone to try to do everything all alone. So, please, if you need help in this class, if you don't know what to do or if you need someone to explain something, ask for help. It's *intelligent* to ask for help. Everything works better that way. We can become a team by helping one another; we can become a community. So, all together now. Let's say it with lots of power."

"It's intelligent to ask for help. No one need to it all alone," the class says.

"Let's look at one last sign today: *We can do more and learn more when we're willing to risk.* Let's say you want to try something new, or talk to someone, or speak up in class. What you want to do might look like a good thing to do, but it can *feel* risky. That often happens to people. We want to do something. Our mind says it would be good to do it. But our feelings say, 'hold on, that's risky!' What then? Should we stop? Sometimes the risk is really too great. We might get hurt or hurt someone else. Then it would be smart to stop, to not do what we thought about doing. But sometimes the risk is really not that great. There is no real danger. It just *feels* risky.

"What we can do, then, is call on our courage and go right through the anxiety. Speak out, if that is what we wanted. Or join a new group. Or jump into the swimming pool. Or whatever it is we wanted to do. The key is to be willing to act, even when it feels risky, even when acting will feel uncomfortable. We need to call up our courage and get started. When we can call up our courage, we can do more and learn more. When we can't call up our courage, we can get stuck, unable to do anything. We may not even be able to think straight about the situation. We may become limited to doing only what feels comfortable.

"But when we are *willing* to call up our courage, we can think about whether there is real danger or not and, if not, we can get going and do it, even though we know that starting will be uncomfortable. We *can* do more and learn more when we are willing to risk. The sign is true.

"Sometimes it helps to have support from others because it's often easier to take a risk when we are not alone. Can anyone here think of a time when having someone to support you made it easier for you to do something?"

Several students raise their hands.

"Did you know that all people have courage? Courage is one of our natural abilities, like speaking and dreaming. Some people can easily call up their courage; others have a more difficult time finding the courage to do things. It may take some practice. Famous people, even movie stars, sometimes get anxious in public. But they are usually good at calling up their courage and getting out in public anyhow. Has anyone here once felt it would be risky to do something, but then called up your courage and did it anyhow?"

Several students raise their hands.

"It's easier to take risks when we can call up the courage inside us, and it's easier too, as I said, when we do not have to go it alone. One other hint: It's also easier to risk if we are willing to accept *not* succeeding. Sometimes it seems so important that we win, or come out on top, or get everything turning out just right that we get nervous before we begin. A part of us does not even want to begin. We forget the simple fact that things do not always turn out the way we like. But if we can accept that fact, if we can remember that people sometimes win and sometimes lose, we won't worry so much about sometimes losing. If we lose, well, we can try again another time. It's usually not the worst thing in the world. And we can then more easily take the risk. How many of you are sometimes afraid of not winning?"

A few students raise their hands.

"Does anyone back off and stop trying in certain situations?"

The room is silent, and not one hand is raised.

"How many would agree that when people can accept winning or losing, however things turn out, they will be less nervous and, if they are not so nervous, might even be more likely to win?"

Most of the students raise their hands.

"In any case, I think you will find this sign is true: We can do more and learn more when we're willing to risk. If there is something good for you to do in this class, I hope you will be willing to do it. Even if it feels a bit risky. Let's repeat the sign together."

"We can do more and learn more when we're willing to risk," reads the class.

"And again," the teacher says, "saying it like you mean it!"

"We can do more and learn more when we're willing to risk!"

"We'll keep these signs posted as reminders for us. From time to time, we'll talk about them again. But now look back at all five. Which ones do you feel good about? Which do you think might help you do good learning in this class?" Pointing to one sign, the teacher asks, "How many feel good about this one?" She counts hands and says, "That's about ten people. How about this sign?"

The teacher tells students the approximate count for each sign, acknowledging the students who raise their hands.

"Now," says the teacher, "I want you to write for me something that you got out of this lesson. You might write endings to one or more of our outcome sentences: I learned . . . , I was surprised . . . , I'm beginning to wonder . . . , I rediscovered . . . , I'm feeling . . . , I promise. . . . Look at the chart for some ideas. Please begin."

The use of truth signs is a strategy I have adopted from Pilon (1991; she calls them philosophy signs). Teachers report that this strategy works well at all grade levels. I myself use truth signs in university courses at the graduate level, though I don't introduce them in quite the same way as the teacher above. Obviously, you must consider the age of your students and your own personality in choosing which signs to introduce and how to introduce them. In my university classes, I usually present and post the five included in the preceding lesson:

- Everyone needs time to think and learn.
- It's okay to make mistakes. That's the way we learn.
- We each learn in our own ways, by our own time clocks.
- It's intelligent to ask for help. No one need do it all alone.
- We can do more and learn more when we're willing to risk.

When introducing the statement about risks to younger students, I make distinctions between a smart risk and a foolish risk. I tell students that I see a smart risk as one that would be good to take, whereas a foolish risk is one that is likely dangerous, or hurtful, or in some way not good for oneself or others. It would be foolish, I remind students, to call up courage and do something that should not be done in the first place. Several teachers have told me that they have asked students to create a chart of smart and foolish risks, and they report that students enjoy this activity.

I have used a discussion of foolish and smart risks to lead into discussions of smoking, drinking, and sex. "Can you think of a time," I usually ask, "when it takes more courage to say no rather than yes?" I then have students role-play situations, aiming to solidify the relationship between risk taking and intelligent choosing.

I recommend using no more than six or seven signs in one classroom. You don't want to dilute the power of the signs. You may want to use signs other than those listed earlier, however. Here are some possibilities:

- Life is not always easy. It can call for a stretch.
- We each must live our own life. No one can do it for us.
- It's not possible to know the full potential of a person.
- Life is one step at a time, one day at a time.
- If it happened, it happened. It can be smart to go on.
- We can be a community: Sometimes all for one and one for all, sometimes live and let live.
- The hardest part of any job can be finishing it.
- You can allow yourself to be your whole, true self.
- There is no final best in the world of humans.

Signs like these communicate important life truths that students and teachers sometimes forget or may not ever have thought about. It is often heartening, reassuring, and strengthening to be reminded of them (see research cited by Hart 1983; Caine and Caine 1991; and Marzano 1992). Cushioning, the strategy discussed on the next page, gives us a meaningful way to carry on such reminders throughout the year.

A Teacher Comments

I have a son, age 7, 2nd grade, and a daughter, just turned 5, preschool. Often at dinner we share information about our days, in particular "what we learned in school." I have discussed the Truth Signs with the children and tried to incorporate them into everyday living. One day last week my children were in the kitchen and I was in another room. I heard my son become exasperated with himself over something he had not done correctly. I then heard my daughter say, "Jed, it's OKAY to make mistakes. That is how we learn." Out of the mouths of babes . . .
—Patrice Bain

Strategy 3.2: Cushioning

Description: Questions or statements designed to reinforce truth signs.

Purpose: To ease students' anxiety in the classroom and help them become more willing to participate fully in learning.

Pilon (1991, pp. 28-29) developed the Cushioning strategy in recognition that posted truth signs alone do not guarantee that students will not feel anxious about learning. As we know, learning takes time, and deep learning often takes a long time. Truth signs are best treated as only a first step in a process of reducing learning anxieties and building students' self-confidence. A steady offering of support is usually necessary if students are to overcome their anxiety about learning. Cushioning is an excellent way to provide that support. There are three steps to Cushioning:

1. Raise awareness of the truth signs. It's usually best to do so by asking questions, such as: "Before we get into our homework review, let me ask you something. Is it okay if someone makes a mistake? Why would that be okay?" Or: "Before we start the discussion I want to ask you something. Is it smart to consider risking today? Why?"

2. Invite students to respond briefly. Accept students' comments without criticism.

3. Wrap up the discussion with a concluding comment similar to those used in the dialogues below, and move promptly into the lesson. Cushioning is not meant to take more than a minute or two.

Here is a short dialogue that shows how the strategy works:

Teacher:	Class, before I ask my questions today, I would like you to guess why I do not care if you make mistakes. Can you guess why that would not bother me at all?
Todd:	Because you want to know how much we know. Mistakes show what we don't know.
Teacher:	Yes, you could say that. Anyone else?
Ginger:	As the sign up there says, it's okay to make mistakes, that's the way we learn.

Teacher:	Yes, that's true. Anyone else?
Frank:	It shows we're trying, risking it, even if we don't know for sure we are right. And we learn more when we're willing to risk.
Teacher:	Yes, all that is true. Our signs remind us of those truths. Now let's get to the questions ...

Notice that the teacher used Cushioning *before* the lesson. Imagine if he waited until *after* a student made a mistake and then asked the class if it was okay to make mistakes. The class might agree, yes it is okay, but the student who just made the error might well be embarrassed to be the cause of such a discussion. Besides, not having begun with that discussion, the lesson may have been proceeding with students unnecessarily anxious about making mistakes. The most powerful use of Cushioning is before lessons begin.

The dialogues below show how the teacher above used the Cushioning strategy with the class on succeeding days.

Day 2

Teacher:	Before we begin this lesson, I want to remind you that no one need learn this material perfectly today. Why do you think I say that?
Bill:	Because it is new material.
Teacher:	Well, it *is* new. But I would say that even about old material. Why is it okay if someone has not learned something perfectly on *any* day?
Sue:	Because we all learn in our own ways, by our own time clocks. It might not be time for us to get something.
Teacher:	Is that true class? (The class agrees, and the teacher continues.) Fine, so go as far as you can. Don't feel bad if you don't understand everything today. Now to our lesson ...

Day 3

The teacher has just asked a question, and Bob has raised his hand:

Teacher:	Bob, before you give your answer, let me ask you something. Is it okay with you if your answer is not the correct answer?
Bob:	Yes, I guess so. Though I wouldn't *like* it!
Teacher:	I can understand that. Yet it is *okay* if you make a mistake, even if you're not entirely happy about it?
Bob:	Yeah, sure.
Teacher:	Can anyone tell us why it would be fine if Bob's answer turns out not to be the correct answer?
Keisha:	Because it's okay to make mistakes. As the sign says, that's the way we learn.
Teacher:	Thanks, Keisha. Sorry for the delay, Bob. Now let me repeat the question and hear your answer.

Day 4

Teacher:	Class, before we begin, let me ask, is it okay for some of you to fully understand this material and for some to still be confused?
Several students:	Yes.
Teacher:	Why it that okay?
Sue:	We all need time to think and learn. Some of us didn't have as much time as we need.
Teacher:	Thank you, Sue. Anyone else?
Cliff:	Some of us might not be very interested in what we're studying.
Teacher:	Thank you, Cliff. Anyone else?

Jim:	We all learn in our own ways, by our own time clocks.
Teacher:	Yes, and how does that truth free us from feeling bad if we don't understand this material? How does it make it okay for some of us to know it and some not to know it?
Tom:	Maybe it wasn't our time to learn it yet.
Teacher:	(No one has another comment.) Thank you, class. It is also possible that you didn't yet have your *way* of learning it. So no one need feel especially great if they learned this already and no one need feel bad if they haven't learned it yet. Learning has a lot has to do with whether your time and way of learning have arrived. Anyhow, let's go at today's work with an accepting, open mind, helping each other as best we can.

Day 5

Teacher:	Today I'd like to begin by asking why you think it's smart to ask a friend for help if you are confused. Anyone?
Mary:	All of us can't ask you all the time.
Denise:	Sometimes it makes me feel good when someone asks me for help.
Teacher:	Yes, thank you. Anyone else?
Carlos:	I'd say because we all learn more when we help one another.
Teacher:	Fine. Just remember that sign. Let's read it all together again.
Teacher and students:	*It's intelligent to ask for help. No one need do it all alone.*
Teacher:	Now for today's lesson . . .

Tips for Using the Cushioning Strategy

I recommend using the Cushioning strategy often, perhaps every day. Pilon (personal communication) recommends keeping Cushioning very brief, a moment or two in passing. Students who need reassurance and confidence in themselves will appreciate the repetition. Others seem not to tire of it. Varying the introductions seems to help keep the process fresh. Here are some possibilities you might want to try:

- Do you have to know everything today? Why not?
- Does anyone here have to be perfect? Why would I not expect that?
- I'd say it's okay if someone forgot what we learned last week. Why might I say that?
- Some of us expect too much of ourselves. How many are sometimes like that? Do any of our signs help us with our expectations?
- It might be unfortunate, but is it okay for someone to have forgotten to bring a notebook today? Why?
- What if someone knows a lot and some others know a little? I'd say that's not important. Which truth signs talk about that?
- I'd say the right answer is not as important as being willing to risk thinking and offering an answer. Can you guess why I'd say that?
- What is the best way to handle a failure? What would be the smart way to react? Why?
- It takes courage to be willing to risk when you are not sure of the outcome. How many would agree? Why?
- No one can ever be me. And I cannot be anyone else. What does that say about how we can best learn here?
- My worth as a person does not depend on how much I know. Why do you think I say that?
- More than right answers, I need the courage to hunt for answers. What sign touches on that?
- It sometimes takes courage to say "I don't know." But sometimes that is the honest answer to a question. What sign relates to that?

Here are some possibilities for closing comments:

- No one knows everything. No one ever will. So relax and just get what you can from this. Okay?
- We are each intelligent about different things. You will find your own intelligence as you go through your days.
- No one in life has to know everything. We help each other. We try to live together as one helpful community.

- All people are unaware of some things. We are just unaware of different things.
- All human beings make mistakes. So, what will you make if you are a human? Mistakes!
- It's not mistakes that are important. It's what we do after we make a mistake.
- Failing at something is not as bad as many people think. Can you imagine what would happen if everyone were always afraid of failing? So let's just forget it and get into today's lesson.
- I'd like you to relax and use your full awareness here. Be a confident learner. There's no need to worry here. So risk jumping in wholeheartedly, thinking only of what you are doing. Trust that the outcome will somehow be okay.

I like Cushioning because it reminds students that they are human and that it's good to be human, to be yourself. Cushioning provides a practical way to help students digest some basic truths of humanness and thereby help them accept themselves—blemishes, tempers, and all—which is often a freeing experience.

A Teacher Comments

I'm using Cushioning throughout my calligraphy unit. It really seems to relax the atmosphere so students can concentrate more on improvement instead of worrying about mistakes.

—Sharon Matti

* * *

Truth Signs and Cushioning reduce a variety of unhealthy pressures on students. They make life easier for students who believe they must be at the top of the class, or who believe they will not be good people unless they do everything immediately and perfectly. Together these two strategies free students' natural curiosities, their natural interest in knowing more about the world and their place in it. Wisely used, these strategies build a sound base for a classroom of active learning.

4 Strategies for Encouraging Beyond Praise and Rewards

Most people enjoy receiving praise and rewards. In proper measure, praise and rewards can motivate us to do our best and help us become confident, self-assured people. They can, however, produce undesirable effects:

• **Addiction.** We can become addicted to praise and rewards. They can become like television programs: providing immediate, easy, and superficial satisfaction while smothering our self-motivation and initiative. Or they're like candy: giving us an instant lift, but then quickly pushing our energy level even lower than before while dulling our taste for more nutritious fare. And like other addictions, praise and rewards can lead to endless desires for more.

• **Unfairness.** Students notice when certain classmates receive lots of hearty praise and rewards while others receive only infrequent praise. *We are not all worthwhile in this class* is the message they receive. And some of them conclude that they are not among the worthy. However innocently we may do so, teachers send these messages, creating a climate that many students feel is unfair to them.

• **Manipulation.** "Look how good the first row is," says the teacher, with the intention of getting all the other rows to straighten up. Many students, however, pick up the more subtle message behind this praise: *It's okay to manipulate people like this to get your way in life.*

• **Puffery.** "Great answer!" the teacher gushes, followed by "Wonderful," "Sensational," "Super," "Amazing," and "Let's give a round of applause to Billy for remembering," omitting the words, "what I just said nine times." Exaggerated praise quickly devalues language and honest relationships. Puffery can also lead to students saying to themselves: "He must think I'm really dumb, expecting me to believe that nonsense" or "She must think I'm really weak if she thinks I need that kind of hype."

Using the strategies in this section, you can support and encourage students without inviting these harmful side-effects. For more discussion on the effects of praise and rewards, see the work of Jere Brophy and others in the Recommended Resources for Chapter 4 on page 187.

Strategy 4.1: "I Appreciate" Message

Description: A statement that communicates something honestly appreciated about students.

Purpose: To remind students that at least one adult appreciates them.

Consider a student who gives an excellent answer to a question. If I wanted to shower praise on that student, I might say, "Very good job, Shirley. The way you phrased your answer was excellent." This is a "you" statement: it says *you* did a good job, and it carries the tone of one person judging the worth of another. If I wanted to give the student a reward, I might say, "Extra credit for that, Shirley." Here the focus is not on the excellence of the work but on payment for the work.

Alternatively, I could make an "I" statement. I might say, "I appreciate the way you phrased your answer, Shirley." Here the intent is to express honest, personal appreciation rather than platitudes or overblown praise. How do people normally express their honest appreciation? Here are some examples I've gathered from teachers:

• Thank you.
• I appreciate that.
• I like the way you said that.
• I sure like your taking that risk.

- Thanks for giving that a try.
- That brings a smile to my face.

"I offer you thanks" is essentially the idea that this response should communicate, a simple offering of honest appreciation for what the person has said or done.

Honest appreciation is not likely to be seen as manipulative, judgmental, or mechanical. And it rarely has negative side-effects so long as all students get their fair share of it. I think we can always find *something* to appreciate in everyone, though we may sometimes have to look harder than we're accustomed to doing. I sometimes think back over a few teaching days to identify students who have missed getting their fair share of appreciation. Then I make a note to myself to look for something about them that I can honestly appreciate.

How does a teacher express honest appreciation if a student gives the *wrong* answer? One option is to say something like "I appreciate your willingness to risk an answer." But more often it is best simply to give the right answer and move on, as the teacher does here with Stan:

Teacher:	What's the capital of New York? (Pause) Stan.
Stan:	New York City.
Teacher:	No, Albany is the capital of New York. What is the capital of Illinois? (Pause) Frank?
Frank:	Springfield.
Teacher:	Yes. What is the capital of . . . ?

Strategy 4.2: "I'm With You" Message

Description: A message that communicates an empathetic acceptance or understanding of a student.

Purpose: To help students understand that they are not alone.

An "I'm With You" Message says to a student, "You are not alone. I'm with you." Here are some examples:

- I might make that same mistake.

- Lots of us feel that way.
- I can tell you're worried about that report.
- I can see how you would do that.
- I think I understand how you feel.
- I'd be proud to be in your shoes.
- I can share your sorrow.
- I understand why you would do that.
- It sounds like that was a great day for you.

Often students will say or do something that makes such a response appropriate, as in this example, which also happens to include an "I Appreciate" Message:

Teacher:	What's the formula for the area of a parallelogram?
Jane:	Uh, is it, uh . . . L x W?
Teacher:	I appreciate that risk, Jane. I could tell you weren't sure and yet you did give it a try. No, the formula for the area of a parallelogram is B x H.

An "I'm With You" Message is another alternative to praise and rewards. It especially benefits students who are feeling alone and inadequate. When they hear a teacher make an "I'm With You" statement, they know the teacher understands what they're going through and is willing to support them.

Strategy 4.3: Attention Without Praise

Description: Giving full attention to a student, as by listening carefully, without offering praise.

Purpose: To support and encourage students without making them overdependent on approval from others.

Sometimes we accidentally fall into praising patterns. Imagine a young student coming to a teacher with a drawing just completed. A caring teacher might easily respond, "What a beautiful picture, Terry!" or "This is a lovely blue tree, Terry," or "You printed your name just perfectly." Yet the student might be quite satisfied with a response that does not include as much praise but still shows that the teacher cares. "I Appreciate" Messages or "I'm With You" Messages provide attention without praise:

- **"I Appreciate" Message.** "I really like this drawing, Terry. Thank you very much for showing it to me!" Or "I really appreciate how carefully you did this drawing."

- **"I'm With You" Message.** "I can see from that big smile on your face, Terry, that you're happy with this drawing! I'd feel the same way if I had drawn it." Or "You seem a bit uncertain about your drawing, Terry. Am I right? Sometimes I don't know quite what to think of my drawings either."

What else can you do to show students that you really care for them, that you notice each of them, that each is an important person—without relying on stock phrases like "good work" and "great job"? Depending on the age and personality of the student and on your own teaching style, you might use:

- **Physical touch.** A pat on the arm, a hug around the shoulder.

- **Eye contact.** A look that communicates full personal attention.

- **Stimulating questions.** "What a bright blue tree, Terry. Did you enjoy doing this?" or "Looks like you used lots of blue in this drawing. Do you like to draw with blue?" or "Thanks, Terry. This is just fine. What would you most like to do next?"

- **Time for the student.** Simply giving a bit of time to the student in whatever way seems right at the moment, as talking about a topic the student initiates, or allowing the student to remain nearby for a moment while you talk with others.

- **Teaching.** Providing instruction or guidance in ways that show you care what the student might next be ready to learn. "I'd like you now to try drawing a face, Terry. Are you ready for that?"

- **Greetings after an absence.** Saying you missed students, that their absence made a difference.

• **Shows of concern.** A response that shows you are concerned about a student's well-being: "You look tired, Terry. Is everything all right with you?"

In short, you might simply show that you care for students and give them some personal attention. Many students, especially young ones, crave such care and attention. You can often provide it without inviting an addiction to praise. You can often give students healthy attention without any praise at all.

Strategy 4.4: Plain Corrects

Description: Straightforwardly informing a student that an answer is correct and then moving on.

Purpose: To confirm correctness without eliciting a distracting emotion.

"Great job! You know your nose is in front of your ears!" It is this kind of overblown praise that Plain Corrects are meant to replace. Plain Corrects are responses like these:

• Yes, that's right.
• Okay.
• Yes, that's just what I wanted.
• Just right.
• Correct.
• Yes, thank you.

A Plain Correct treats students like intelligent, dignified people who prefer straight talk to overstatements. It cleanly gives a message: *Your answer was correct. Let's move on.* A Plain Correct is a judgment, but unlike praise, which often feels like a judgment of one's self, a Plain Correct is simply a judgment of a response. It is an assessment by an expert, the teacher, of the accuracy of an answer and, as such, is quite helpful. The student now knows that the answer given is correct.

When you respond to students with Plain Corrects, a response Pilon (1991) recommends, you are serving as an efficient answer key: "Yes, you have that one right. Now to the next one . . . " You do not stir up emotions that might distract students from the intellectual work of learning.

Strategy 4.5: Plain Incorrects

Description: Straightforwardly informing a student that an answer is not correct and then moving on.

Purpose: To inform students that an answer is incorrect without eliciting any distracting emotion.

Plain Incorrects, another type of response recommended by Pilon (1991), are very much like Plain Corrects:

- No, the correct answer is Louisiana Purchase.
- No, that's not what I was wanting. Please use adjectives like those on the board.
- You had the first name right. The correct answer is Thomas Jefferson.
- That's an answer for the kidney. Bile is the answer for the stomach.

With a Plain Incorrect, you simply give expert responses to students and then move on. There is no hint in the response that students are so fragile they cannot handle making factual errors.

On Combining Responses

It is sometimes appropriate to combine judgments of correctness with "I Appreciate" Messages and "I'm With You" Messages:

- That's right, Cleo. And I appreciate your volunteering.
- Yes, Sheila. I know that was a tough problem for you to solve.
- No, Bob. The answer is nine. I can tell you're disappointed you missed that one, but there's always next time.
- No, the answer is southwest. By the way, Tim, I'm glad you gave your answer with power in your voice.

On Drawing Out Answers from Students

One common teaching practice is to follow an incorrect student response with a drawing-out process: "No, not New York City; the capital of New York state starts with the letter A. Can you guess? Want another hint?" This practice puts the student on the spot and may cause embarrassment or shame. It is not a particularly good strategy for promoting dignity in the classroom. Moreover, it slows the quick pace

I recommend for today's students. If you're striving for quick-paced lessons, I recommend just giving the right answer and moving on.

On Calling on a Second Student

Calling on a second student to answer a question that another student has just answered incorrectly is a common teaching practice; however, I do not recommend it. It often makes the first student feel inferior to the student who eventually gives the correct answer. In my classes, I want to avoid pitting one student against another. Since I already have asked the question, all students have had a chance to think about the answer, so I may as well keep them all interested by giving them the correct answer and then offering another question for all students to consider.

Strategy 4.6: Silent Response

Description: Making a mental note of a student error or problem, but leaving until later the consideration of what, if anything, is to be done about it.

Purpose: To avoid responding in unproductive ways to students' mistakes.

Sometimes the best response a teacher can make is no response—other than a mental note to oneself. For instance, let's say one of your students is reporting work for his group. Several times during his oral report he says "ain't" and "ain't not." What should your response as a teacher be? No response, other than to make a mental note that he and perhaps others in the class need more practice saying "isn't" and "is not."

Let's look at another example: A student turns in a report that confuses *too* and *to*. Should a teacher mark that error? If the teacher does so, two consequences are predictable. First, odd as it may seem, the student will probably continue making the error. Most teachers have learned that marking errors rarely changes future behavior. Second, the student will be less willing to keep writing anything for anybody, even himself. Students rarely enjoy activities that are likely to lead to corrections.

What is the alternative here? A Silent Response. Keep your observation of the error a secret. Remember the error and perhaps make a note to create an appropriate mini-lesson another day for the whole class or a small group. And at that time, do not say, "We need to review *too* and *to* because we have not yet mastered them." Do not say anything that may communicate to students, *You should have already learned this.* Such a message is unnecessary and may cause students to become discouraged. Simply teach the lesson as if it had never been taught in that class. Here, for instance, is one way you might approach the *too* versus *to* lesson:

> "Here on the board are examples of *too*, t-o-o, and *to*, t-o, used correctly in a sentence. Because they sound alike, it's easy to confuse these words. I want each of you to please write a pair of sentences on scrap paper. In one, use *too*, t-o-o, correctly. In the other, use *to*, t-o, correctly. Perhaps write about something that recently happened to you.
>
> "Now, please share your sentences with a partner. Check to see that both words are correctly used in the sentences. If you and your partner are both unsure about what is correct, ask another pair of students for help.

The teacher in this example could focus a second round of practice on a different topic: "Now write sentences that deal with pets or animals." For fun and variety, the teacher could even shift the lesson content: "Here now are two math problems. Work them out alone and then see if you and your partner got the same answer. If not, help each other. If you both got the answers, try making up a harder problem for each other."

In short, we need not point out an error to get students to learn. We can simply teach a lesson about the topic again. As long as the lesson has a quick pace, it will be an easy review for students who already understand and, for those who do not, a chance to learn in a climate without overtones of failure.

It's not always necessary to keep silent about errors, of course. Once teachers and students have built solid, accepting relationships, they usually do not mind having someone point out the occasional error. If you're unsure about the strength of your relationship with your students and of your students' relationships with one another, then I recommend using the Silent Response. It is the medicine most likely to have the least harmful side effects.

Strategy 4.7: Praise and Rewards for All —————————

Description: Praise or rewards offered to the group as a whole.

Purpose: To encourage a group without slighting any student and to build group unity.

One of the biggest drawbacks of praise and rewards in the classroom is that some students receive them often, others rarely. Worse yet, those who do not receive praise or rewards begin to think of themselves as "not good enough." When a teacher says "Good answer" to one of the high-achieving students in the class, many other students are thinking, "I only wish I were like that kid, not like me." Sensitivity to the potential hurt to students sometimes causes teachers to lavish praise and rewards on all. But students are aware beings. They can distinguish contrived, undeserved praise or inflated reward from the real thing.

I have heard it argued that given the downside of praise and rewards we should do away with them entirely. I would not go that far. In fact, I recommend praise and rewards when they can honestly be given to all:

• "This group is making great progress. It's a pleasure for me to work with you."

• "Let's give ourselves a hand for the way we handled today's lesson."

• "You all are working so well together! I told the principal today how special you are."

• "This class is going so well I'm giving you all a treat today."

• "What a good group this is. Even though that material was hard, you folks stuck with it. I admire your perseverance."

• "We did it right on time! This sure is a powerful bunch, isn't it!"

• "I'm proud that one of our own classmates, Nicky, won first prize. And I'm proud of the way you people supported Nicky. So I brought an apple today for everyone in honor of Nicky." (Even when rewards cannot be distributed equally, I like to make sure everyone gets something.)

No one loses when praise and rewards are honest and directed to the group as a whole. There's no envy, no one left out. Group rewards also foster feelings of community. Not all group praise and rewards are equally valuable, however. The strategy can be used manipulatively, as when a teacher offers a reward only when students do what the teacher wants. A class party on Friday because of diligent work all week falls in that category. The motive of a teacher can be less to bring delight to students, to show appreciation, to share good feelings with the class than to shape the future behavior of students. Not only is this motive less generous, it bolsters the tendency some students have to manipulate others.

I prefer not to make group praise or rewards contingent on student behavior. I do not like to announce that *if* students do this or that they will get a reward. I prefer to give students a model of someone who likes to bring joy into others' lives, rather than a model of someone who expects people to earn everything they receive. I like to give praise and rewards to all especially because people not earning much are often those most in need of more joy in their lives.

Strategy 4.8: Honest Delight

Description: A statement expressing spontaneous delight with a student.

Purpose: To allow oneself to be spontaneously expressive. Also, to demonstrate the reality that people have the ability to delight others.

The preceding strategies give us replacements for individual praise. Students get supportive feedback and encouragement and we avoid problems of addiction, unfairness, manipulation, and puffery. Does that mean that you have to suppress your spontaneous delight in the classroom? No, it does not. I can, for example, hear myself saying:

- I really like the colors in that shirt, Tom.
- Good risk taking, Stu.
- What bright eyes you have today, Zack.
- That was a really neat paper you wrote yesterday, Lois.
- What good initiative you took, Jim.
- I was delighted to see how you stuck with your friend, Terry.
- You were truthful, and that was not easy, Sam. I was very happy to see that.
- Great answer, Gloria. Very creative.

I call these Honest Delights. They are simply expressions of my spontaneous joy or delight; they are not intended to uplift the student but to express my feelings. I could not be genuine without being willing to express such reactions. And I believe teachers should be genuine.

Honest Delights are warmer, more infused with emotional energy than "I Appreciate" Messages. But they are not exaggerated or artificial, nor are they used to manipulate others to behave in certain ways. Furthermore, Honest Delights are not to be prolonged to the point that they embarrass a student or cause other students to become envious. Honest Delights are spontaneous, instantaneous. They are expressed and then let go.

Honest Delights are especially appropriate for young students, because these children have a special need to know they can bring delight to the world around them. Perhaps that is why most adults naturally smile at young children. It is nature's way of eliciting the response those youngsters need.

As with "I Appreciate" Messages, we must take care not to neglect some students when we distribute our Honest Delights. This is not too difficult, since delights need not be based solely on academic performance. We can find something in every student that will delight us if we wait long enough and look closely enough. To do this, I sometimes recommend making a list of students and checking the name after offering an honest delight, so as to notice which students are not getting a fair share. We can then be on the lookout for things about the person that honestly delight us.

Not that such responses must be distributed absolutely equally. Sooner or later students must learn that some people elicit a more positive response from people than do others. That's a fact of life. Having a bit of imbalance in the distribution of Honest Delights seems to me acceptable *as long as* every student experiences some of them and no student gets too many. It is the extremes we must guard against. It seems to me far different to have some rich folk in a town of generally well off people than to have some extremely wealthy people and others who have not enough for food and shelter.

Each teacher will find different delights in students. Almost any delight is fine, as long as it is *honestly* delightful to the teacher and not embarrassing to the student or his peers: an article of clothing, the confidence with which a student strides, progress in holding a temper, promptness, shining hair, wise caution or adventurousness, even great answers and super projects, as in the last two items listed above.

Strategy 4.9: DESCA Inspirations

Description: Teacher comments to stir appreciation of the inherent *dignity* of all students; appropriate personal *energy*; intelligent *self-management*; healthful *community* relationships; and searching, open *awareness*.

Purpose: To inspire new growth in dignity, energy, self-management, community, and awareness (DESCA).

I've already suggested that you need not respond to everything students say or do. If a student flaunts his good looks and clothing, for example, you might well not say you appreciate today's new outfit. You might, indeed, generally avoid comments about clothing and looks because such comments can encourage attention to superficial matters and, when overheard by others, can distress those less able to display an attractive appearance.

Similarly, you may choose not to shower praise on all superior work. Too much appreciation can complicate future expectations and current humility. I think of the outstanding high school students who go to top colleges and attempt suicide after discovering that they are no longer the top students in their class. Some students define their worth in terms of what they produce, just as some adults define their goodness in terms of social status or possessions. When such students do excellent work and we say we are delighted, we risk reinforcing that definition. We risk, too, hardening an assumption that if they cannot produce they will be less worthy human beings.

We may generally want to avoid comments about excellent products when we sense that such comments put students who are not producing excellent work at a disadvantage. These students are equally deserving of our respect and appreciation. Democracy calls for a reasonable amount of equality among citizens. Besides, I believe the way we conduct our lives is often more important than the products of work. I believe we need to encourage students to cultivate such habits as calling up their courage, sticking to tough tasks, thinking through issues, and lending a hand to strangers.

I try not to miss the opportunity to comment on instances when students strive to use their full potential or to embrace their dignity as human beings. As I explained in the Introduction, one of my goals as a teacher is to inspire dignity, energy, self-management, community, and awareness: DESCA. Below are some examples of how a teacher might use "I Appreciate" Messages and "I'm With You" Messages to inspire these five qualities. Such comments should be distributed widely among students, not restricted to only a few. If I sense that some students need an extra dose of this kind of support, I talk privately to them, aiming to give them what they need and to avoid making other students envious of the attention I'm giving them.

"I Appreciate" Messages That Inspire DESCA

Dignity
- I really like the way you just spoke up for yourself.
- I enjoy the confidence you are showing.
- I like the way you defended your friend.
- I like how you said it like you meant it.
- I sure appreciate the way you look straight in people's eyes.

Energy
- I like it when you stick to it.
- I like it when you use your brain power.
- I like it when you pace yourself.
- I like it when you speak with energy.
- I like it when you go one more step when you are ready to give up.

Self-Management
- I like it when you organize your own papers neatly.
- I like it when you make a time plan.
- I like it when you reach down for your ability to persist when you need it.
- I like it when you think it out for yourself.
- I like it when you ask for help when you need it.

Community
- I like it when you respect the differences in others.
- I like it when you find something to appreciate in people so different from you.
- I like it when you lend a hand.
- I like it when you listen so well to others.
- I like it when you do more than your share of the work without being asked.

Awareness
- Thank you very much for being so alert.
- Thank you very much for reading with an open mind.

- Thank you very much for bringing your attention back when it drifted.
- Thank you very much for ignoring the distractions outside.
- Thank you very much for noticing that someone needed help.

"I'm With You" Messages That Inspire DESCA

Dignity
- I can imagine how you felt after speaking up that way.
- I'm also proud of myself when I go that extra mile.
- I think I know how you felt when you insisted on your rights.
- It's sometimes hard, isn't it, to call on your willpower?
- There was a time when I, too, could not get all the courage I wanted.

Energy
- I need rest too.
- I enjoy moving about too.
- I'm like you when it comes to taking initiative.
- It's not easy to eat well all the time, is it?
- I, too, sometimes have trouble getting myself up after I'm too down.

Self-Management
- I, too, have trouble knowing when to speak up and when to say nothing.
- We can each tell what is true for us, can't we?
- I understand how you knew when you had enough.
- Sometimes we must look twice to see what needs to be done, don't we?
- I, too, must sometimes remind myself not to be negative.

Community
- I understand how you felt about cleaning up a mess you didn't make.
- It's fun to cheer people on, isn't it?
- I, too, like to show others my appreciation.
- You feel good when you reach out to newcomers, don't you?
- It feels good to me, too, when I can stand up for our class.

Awareness
- I, too, sometimes do not manage myself as well as I want to.
- I, too, sometimes go too fast without noticing it.
- I, too, sometimes think back over the day and wonder what I should do next time.
- I, too, sometimes need to pull myself out of dullness.
- I, too, sometimes wonder about my feelings.

5 Strategies for Raising Standards of Excellence

I believe all people have within themselves the capacity to appreciate excellence. Even the young man who does the sloppiest work for me recognizes excellent athletic play and good battle plans. What is it that moves students to recognize and strive for that same kind of excellence in their schoolwork?

• **Success** plays a part. Students who repeatedly fail to achieve excellence tend to give up. They think to themselves, "I can't win, so why even try? I'll just put in enough effort to stay out of trouble."

• **Feelings of importance** play a part. Students do better at tasks that are important to them.

• **Absence of high anxiety** plays a part. Too much anxiety is crippling. It can freeze the mind. When students are afraid of making a mistake or feel they must learn something right now, their minds can stop cold.

• **Choice in ways of working** plays a part. Students who are allowed to do some things their own way are more likely to do an excellent job than students who are forced to do things the way someone else wants them to.

• **Personal time clocks** make a difference. When students can do a job at a time that is right for them and at their own speed, they are more likely to do excellent work than if they have to do that job in a shorter or longer time or when they're not ready for it.

• **Strong leadership** often inspires excellent work. The high energy and constant support of a strong leader can motivate many students to do remarkably excellent work.

• **The high energy and constant support of a strong group** can bring students to excellence. It's the power of teamwork.

Offering rewards for top performance is one of the least effective ways to encourage students to strive for excellence. Rewards and recognition keep good workers working, but they generally don't drive mediocre and poor workers toward excellence. Doling out penalties for poor performance is probably the worst thing a teacher who cares about excellence can do. The threat of penalties rarely brings out people's best efforts, especially over the long run. Few students commit themselves to personal standards of excellence because of scoldings and punishments. In this chapter, we'll look not at issues of instruction but at strategies that more generally bring students toward excellent workmanship.

Strategy 5.1: Learning Challenge

Description: An assignment posed as a challenge or an opportunity, not as a chore or burden.

Purpose: To inspire high-energy work.

Many young people today could use more challenges. A challenge, as I use the term here, is not a chore or burden, but an exciting, adventurous, stretching opportunity, a chance to be undaunted by obstacles, to reach and conquer. A good challenge enlivens students. Let's look at some excerpts from a lesson:

> "How many of you have ever faced a really tough challenge and overcome it? Maybe trying something new, or working hard at something, or resisting doing something you really wanted to do but knew was not smart to do. Perhaps you needed grit, or spunk, or just plain determination, or lots of courage. Anyone willing to tell us about a time you succeeded at something that

was a real challenge to you, though it may not have been a challenge to other people?

"Those of you who overcame your challenges, how many found it invigorating, good for you? How many found it good for you even when you were not able to succeed, just because you *accepted* the challenge?

"Most of us enjoy a good challenge. I would like to invite you to undertake more challenges in this class. Look at the next unit we will study, the one we introduced yesterday. I'd like to see if some of you feel up to a challenge with that unit.

"One challenge, for example, would be to target a certain number of difficult items to master by a certain date. Then really go for it. You might even set an early deadline, if that will add zest to your challenge.

"Another challenge might be to create something related to the material in the unit. You could challenge yourself to build something or dramatize certain events in a really masterful way.

"Or you might challenge yourself to study the standard material but handle it in a new way, a way that is not normal for you, a way that will get you stretching your skills and talents or, maybe, your relationships.

"Can anyone think of other challenges we could mention? Perhaps we can dream up some more as we discuss the material today.

"Some of you may not feel up to a challenge right now. I would say it is smart not to undertake a challenge that is not right for you, and smart not to undertake a challenge when the time is not right for you. Can anyone guess why I say this? . . . We can all still participate in the challenge activities, though. In this unit, the job of those of us without a challenge is to be cheerleaders for the others. So take some time and think about whether you can find a challenge for yourself in the unit ahead or if you prefer to be a cheerleader, to support and encourage the challengers.

"If you do accept a challenge, I challenge you to strive fully, really go for it, give it your all. Then, whatever the outcome, *accept* it fully, take what you get without regrets. We all win some and lose some. That's life!"

Organizing for Challenge

In Chapter 8, I suggest that students form support groups of perhaps four students who sit together every day for a month or more to help one another. If such groups are formed, students without challenges can be the cheerleaders for the members of their group who have accepted challenges. They can encourage the challengers, ask about progress, even phone them after school to boost their confidence. Consider leading a discussion on the importance of people having cheerleaders in their lives, how much easier it is to persist through difficulties when we do not go it alone, how much more we can accomplish when we are cheered on, and what kind of cheering works best for people.

What Makes for an Appropriate Challenge?

• The timing is right. It must be the right time for that person. Sometimes an extra challenge is the last thing a person needs.

• The level of the challenge is right. The possibility of success must be neither too high nor too low, and what constitutes too high and too low should be clearly defined, preferably by the person being challenged.

• The challenge is freely accepted. A challenge unwillingly accepted will likely be a burden and a chore. An appropriate challenge requires willing, personal commitment.

• The acceptance is invigorating, empowering. An appropriate challenge ignites new motivation and new energy, yet does not overwhelm students. One is proud of it, glad to have it.

The challenge that is always appropriate for us is the challenge to be our best self, the self that, deep down, we know we want to be.

Who Reaps the Rewards of Challenges?

Everyone in the class should be rewarded in some way. Public appreciation for only the winners slights, even depreciates, the students who did not meet their challenges. Similarly, recognizing only the students who undertook a challenge can diminish those who chose "not now," those who may wisely have opted out. If there is to be applause, I recommend it be for all, for the class community: "Let's give ourselves a hand for the way we helped one another with those challenges!"

Here's how a 2nd grade teacher reviewed challenges with her class, using four rounds of applause:

> "Let's see how our challenge went. First of all, how many are still working on their challenges, are not ready to stop yet? Our job of course will be to continue cheering those folks on. Please stand, persisters! Let's give these folks a hand for their persistence!" The class applauds.

"How many were brave enough to undertake a challenge that was not easy for you, whether or not you were successful so far? Please stand and show us your courageous faces. Let's give those folks a round of applause!" The class applauds.

"How many were smart enough not to undertake a challenge at this time, perhaps because it seemed not the right time or not the right challenge for you? Please stand and show us your wise faces. Let's give those folks a rousing round of applause!" The class applauds.

"How many of you enjoyed getting cheered on by others or did some cheering or at least thought about cheering? Everyone please stand. Everyone, let's stand tall and cheerful and give ourselves a hand! I'd say we all did a good job!" The class applauds.

Strategy 5.2: Inspiring Statement

Description: A statement that cheers students on to do their best work.

Purpose: To ignite the power of students to meet their challenges.

Imagine a teacher saying to a class, "I care very much that you succeed in the future. I want you prepared to be a winner in your course work next year. I want you to get this material down cold. Learn it backwards and forwards. Let's get to it!"

As all coaches know, sometimes saying the right thing at the right time can move people to surpass their own expectations, to reach deep down and make those extra efforts. Inspiration has to do with bringing out the *spirit,* the vital force, within us. Once that inner power, or self-motivation, is ignited, people push themselves to do their best.

If you are unpracticed in cheering students on, know that the most effective Inspiring Statements are rooted in genuine, respectful care. Sometimes, especially with older students, these statements are best made privately. Inspiring Statements stir up the best in others. They reach deep and say, in effect, "I'm with you. I want this for you. Working together, we can do the job." They do not say, "Do this for me. I'm insisting on it. It is required." They pull, not push, students:

• Pushing: "I want you all to master this material. It is extremely important. I will have no student of mine leaving here without knowing this. You must learn it and learn it well to pass this class."

• Pulling: "You will really need this material. I'm committed to doing whatever I can to make sure you get it and get it well. Are you willing to come with me and go for it? It will be a challenge. Let's do it!"

The care of one person for another ignites the deep inner power that leads to the most inspired efforts. And if the care is mutual, if the students also care for the teacher, the inspiration flows along a highly-charged path: "We are in this together. Yet I can't do the learning for you. You must do it. By now you know how much I care for you. If for no other reason, learn this for me. I want you to master this material perfectly. I want to be proud for you. Let's show the world we can do it. Here we go."

I recently heard about an elementary school principal in Illinois, Frank Beczkala, who wanted to inspire students to do more reading. "If every student reads more," he announced, "I, who am deathly afraid of high places, will stand on the roof of this building and read out loud a story to those assembled below." The students met the challenge. And so did he.

Strategy 5.3: High Expectations

Description: Maintaining an expectation that students will do excellent work, even when there is not yet evidence that they will do so.

Purpose: To take advantage of the power of expectations.

As a teacher, I never want to lay negative expectations on my students. When, for example, I give an assignment, I fully expect all will do it, and do it with verve and diligence. When some do not, I fully expect that those students had good reason not to and, next time I give an assignment, all will *then* do it. I never assume any student lacks in personal willingness to learn, for I believe that when we expect the best we are more likely to get the best. If I were to expect my students not to study unless I gave them rewards and punishments, grades and tests, reminders and scoldings, they would likely oblige me.

It is valuable to keep expecting willing, self-motivated work from students. It is, I believe, one of a teacher's most influential, far-reaching strategies. If you have trouble with this strategy, consider these ideas:

• Remind yourself that students probably pursue their after-school games and interests with spirit and dedication. Remind yourself that these young people do have the capacity for diligence and that it might well be possible to bring that self-motivation into the classroom. Perhaps remind yourself, too, of the advantages in expecting that self-motivation to increasingly show up in the classroom.

• To activate students' powers of self-motivation, occasionally ask students about what they do when they're not in school: their hobbies, teams, social activities, the events they really care about. Observe the change in their energy level when they talk about these activities.

• Try the New or Good Invitation strategy (discussed in Chapter 6 on page 89). Use a few minutes at the start of some classes to ask, "Is there anything new or good in your lives? Has anybody won a prize, made a new friend, lost a hat?" Invite a few students to comment. This verbal show and tell encourages students to share their personal realities. It also builds community and gives all students a chance to shine. And it makes it easier for you to know and appreciate the unique humanness of each student.

• Notice that the activities in an Action Flow Lesson get students working without any need for rewards or threats. Diligent, self-motivated work is possible. Assume that if you find enough strategies you can steadily expand the time students will spend working that way. Make real for yourself the possibility of seeing all students working willingly, with persistent self-motivation.

• Consider that few students want to be poor readers, clumsy calculators, ignorant of what goes on in the world. My experience tells me that students *do* want to be skillful and informed in life. They see no advantage to being unskilled and ignorant. Their natural motives support learning, though many of them simply do not know how to learn in ways that fit their individual human needs.

• Write affirmations or visualization statements. Each day write a statement that affirms the expectation that you and your students will find a way for learning to take place with full cooperation and self-sustaining energies. Choose words that make you feel positive, perhaps something like this: "I see my students working more and more willingly, more and more enthusiastically." As you write, visualize students studying that way. The more vivid and colorful your visualization, the sooner you are likely to see it in the classroom.

Strategy 5.4: DESCA Challenges

Description: Challenges that stretch students' capacity to live with full *dignity*, high *energy*, wise *self-management*, in respectful *community*, or with open *awareness* (DESCA).

Purpose: To advance those human capacities.

___

You can empower students profoundly by sprinkling lessons with nondemanding but stimulating challenges along the five themes of DESCA:

Dignity. Please stand tall when you make that announcement. When someone is being teased, I'd like to see more people aiming to defend the person. Look people in the eye. Speak up for yourself. Show your willpower. Refuse to be put down. Say it like you mean it. Walk away when people are gossiping hurtfully. Reach down for your courage. Stand up for what you believe in. Move ahead with confidence. Act with authority. Sit tall in your chair. Show your inner strength. Show you can take it. Remember, mistakes do not touch your dignity. Respect your ways, your time clock. Even if it feels risky, please call up your courage and do what you think best.

Energy. Please keep yourself active, but take care not to set a pace that's too hectic. Stick to it. Apply your full self to the job. Use all your brain power. Reach down for the ability to persist. Make sure you get plenty of sleep. Eat well. Pace yourself. When you think you are ready to give up, take one more step. Put your all into it. Make sure you get enough exercise. Let yourself shine. Walk briskly. Get yourself ready. Take initiative. Speak with energy. Move right along. Relax now to be strong later. Use your whole self. Let the joy of living show in every step you take. Call up your aliveness. Go for it.

Self-Management. Please control your impulses. Rest when you need to rest. Take care of leftover tasks. Think things through for yourself. Go past the first idea. Ask for help when you need it. You will know what's right. You can think for yourself. You will know what to do. You will notice when something needs to be done. Tell yourself you do not have to be negative. Proceed by your own time clock. When you feel low, get up and do something. When you are angry, slowly count to ten. Start yourself with willpower. Practice starting immediately. Put things aside. Stop yourself with willpower. Practice stopping immediately. Take control of your behavior. Organize your papers. Manage your own time. Look ahead and plan.

Community. Please respect the differences in others. Be all for one, one for all. Listen to others. Help clean up. Do more than your share. Cheer people on. Show your appreciation. Accept compliments. Care for those who need it. Reach out to newcomers. Practice going out of your way for others. Look for the good in everyone. Accept all people for being who they are. Tell people when you do not understand. Be honest here. Stand up for our group. Let us know when we make mistakes. Think about how we can do better at being one supportive community. Do something extra at home. Help your family. Do something good for the community. Pick up trash when you see it. Ask family members how you can help them. Connect to someone new.

Awareness. Please keep alert. Read with an open mind. Call up your intelligence. Reach for your full creativity. When your attention drifts, bring it back, stay alert. Practice ignoring distractions. Recall past ideas. Notice when someone needs help. Notice nonverbal messages. Focus your attention. Look for the details. Open your mind to big ideas. Wonder what else. Notice your feelings. Enjoy hearing, seeing, feeling, smelling, tasting. Keep a log of your thoughts, dreams, feelings. Ask others about their ideas. Look below the surface. Notice how your days are going. Notice what is being left undone. Closely study colors and sounds. Notice when your thinking becomes sluggish. Notice where feelings show up in your body. Notice what's going on around you. When you are going too fast, back off. Notice how your body feels. End each day by telling yourself what you liked about that day and what you might do differently another time.

Another Option: Assignments with Choice

Teachers often assign homework that offers students little choice in what to do: "Do the first ten problems on page 36." "Read Chapter 10 and be ready for a test on it." Such assignments miss valuable opportunities, especially the opportunity to individualize instruction somewhat and the opportunity to train students in responsible self-management.

Assignments with Choice invite the bright or interested student to do more work, something students rarely do when assignments are

without choice. More important, making choice part of every homework assignment gives students real practice in learning to make wise
choices for themselves. I recommend periodically talking to students
about the idea of making choices and how it fits in with doing homework. If you are interested in pursuing the idea of Assignments with
Choice, turn to page 131 in Chapter 10, where you'll find a more
complete explanation of this strategy.

6 Strategies for Beginning a Class

There are many effective ways to begin a class. One of the easiest is the Voting strategy, which was discussed in Chapter 2 (see page 30). It involves simply asking a few questions to which students can respond by raising their hands. Questions like these help break the ice and focus the class's attention:

- How many of you have had a good day so far?
- How many were surprised by the sudden rain?
- How many just love rainy days?
- Is anyone wearing something new today?
- How many remember where we left off yesterday's lesson?

Here are five other strategies I often use to begin a class, sometimes in combination, sometimes by themselves.

Strategy 6.1: Lesson Agreement

Description: Outlining the lesson planned and inviting student agreement.

Purpose: To maximize student cooperation.

You might ask for agreement in this manner: "Today I plan to start with our homework. Then I thought we might begin our discussion on France. After that, there would be time for your group project work. If time remains, we could do some map work. How does that sound? Can we agree on that plan?" Some students may have suggestions for changing the plan, but you decide whether the suggestions are worthwhile. You have final responsibility. The intent here is not to expect all to agree, but to use a moment or two to demonstrate respect for student intelligence, invite collaboration, and hear suggestions, so the class moves ahead with maximum cooperation.

You may present the plan in writing instead of orally—on the chalkboard, for instance. For older students, you might ask for agreement with a longer plan of a week or more, perhaps even a plan for the whole course.

The Lesson Agreement strategy is similar to what Madeline Hunter (1984) calls an "anticipatory set." Both strategies get students looking forward to the lesson ahead. The difference is simply in the invitation to accept the plan that is included here. Asking the class "Is that okay with you?" is, of course, asking them to become a participant in the work ahead.

Strategy 6.2: Immediate Work Assignment

Description: Work students handle as soon as they enter the classroom.

Purpose: To get students productively involved at the very beginning of class.

Many teachers instruct students to begin working on an assignment as soon as they enter the room, not to wait until the teacher calls the class to order. Assignments that are appropriate for beginning a class include:

• Writing in journals, perhaps in response to a posted quotation of the day.
• Working on problems written on the chalkboard.
• Sitting in pairs and checking each other's homework, perhaps against a posted answer key.
• Starting work on individual tasks, worksheets, or learning center activities.

The idea is to create immediate work so students waste no time and lose no energy waiting for activities to get underway. This strategy also gives you time for tasks such as preparing lesson materials, taking attendance, and consulting with individual students.

Strategy 6.3: Motivating Question

Description: A question focusing student attention and inspiring student thinking.

Purpose: To generate student interest in a lesson and to focus their attention.

Some teachers open lessons with a question to promote thinking and focus attention on the lesson ahead. Once student interest is awakened, the lesson then proceeds more easily. Here are several examples of Motivating Questions:

• Can you name an animal that carries its young for more than a year before giving birth?
• What do you know about the reasons for the Civil War?
• Would anyone like to estimate how much faster a dime falls than a nickel?

Sometimes the question may refer to an earlier lesson. For instance: What did we say last time about a good diet? And using the Question, All Write strategy after a Motivating Question often gets students ready to jump into a topic.

Strategy 6.4: New or Good Invitation

Description: Inviting a class to share events in their lives that are new or good.

Purpose: To focus student attention and build a healthy community climate.

From Jackins (1974) I've learned the value of starting meetings by asking "Who can tell us something new or good in your life?" When I first use this strategy with a class, I usually help students along with some prompts. For instance, I ask: "Has anyone received a compliment? Bought a new car? Anything good happen at home or school?" Whatever students say, then, I accept, usually by saying something like "Thank you for sharing that" or "I can appreciate that." After a few moments, I move into the day's lesson.

The intent here is not to raise issues for discussion, although it sometimes is wise to allow a discussion to emerge, as when a student raises an issue important to all. The intent is to give students a few moments to share the interesting, happy, or sad events in their lives. This strategy allows students who may not shine in academic areas to talk about other areas of their lives—being on a winning baseball team, for example. It allows students who are experiencing anguish—over the death of a pet, perhaps—to vent their feelings. In many ways, this strategy brings a class together in deeper and more expansive appreciation of one another. And when used to open a class, it usually brings student attention fully into the classroom.

Strategy 6.5: Risk Reminder

Description: Reminding students that learning often involves risks, with perhaps some encouragement to consider risking in class today.

Purpose: To encourage students to stretch beyond easy learning.

When the lesson ahead may be challenging, I sometimes begin class in this way: "How many of you are up for a risk today? How many are ready to do some good thinking? We have a tricky lesson today, an important one. Can you stretch yourself for it?"

One of the truth signs recommended in Chapter 3 talks about taking risks: *We can do more and learn more when we are willing to risk.* I find it useful to remind students of the need to sometimes reach beyond a comfort zone, to call up courage and plunge into what may be a difficult experience. I use the Risk Reminder strategy for that purpose.

I also use this strategy in discussions to encourage students to reach for new learnings. Rather than ask who is willing to give an answer, which tends to get the same old talkers volunteering, I ask this question: "How many would be willing to risk giving an answer?" I say "How many" rather than "Who" because this phrasing prompts more students to volunteer. And I say "risk an answer" rather than "give an answer" to better emphasize that open-minded, deep thinking and full participation often go hand in hand with risking.

I often use the Cushioning strategy along with Risk Reminders. For instance, I may ask, "Would it be okay if some choose not to risk sharing right now?" "Sure," students usually say, "We each have our own ways and time clocks. Besides, some of us may need more time to think."

7 **Strategies for Concluding a Class**

No two classes are the same. Each has its own rhythm and momentum. But all classes must end at some point. Some are best ended like a chapter in the middle of a book, with a pause that promises there is more to come. Others are best ended with a definite wrap-up experience of some kind, perhaps to help students review while the experience is still fresh. Two strategies introduced in Chapter 2 are particularly effective for providing this kind of wrap-up experience:

• **The Outcome Sentences strategy.** When students' grasp of a variety of understandings is especially important to the day's lesson, I often use the Outcome Sentences strategy. For instance, I may point to a chart showing phrases such as *I learned . . .* , *I rediscovered . . .* , *I was surprised . . .* , *I'm beginning to wonder. . . .* Then I say, "Think back over the material we just covered. See what understandings you can draw from it for yourself. Write a few sentences, perhaps starting with phrases like these on the chart."

After allowing a few minutes for students to write their ideas, I invite a few volunteers to read aloud one of their outcome sentences. Sometimes I use the Whip Around, Pass Option strategy, perhaps asking a row of students to read one of their statements. Or I might simply ask students to file their notes in a personal portfolio. (See page 25 for more information on the Outcome Sentences strategy.)

• **The Review Test strategy.** For this strategy, I give one question to the whole class, students write answers at their desks, and then I give the correct answer. Students check their work on each question before hearing the next question. The process continues through a series of such questions. If single correct answers to questions exist, as with math or spelling, I usually write correct answers on the chalkboard, so students' thinking is minimally disturbed by classroom talk. If answers are more complex or subjective, I either give one correct answer or invite a few students to share their answers.

I make sure the pace of the lesson is rapid enough to keep awareness and energy high. I minimize discussion, and when I notice that some students don't quite understand a question, I make the next question overlap an earlier question, so students learn from the review practice.

A Review Test could be used early in a lesson to go over prior learnings and at the end of a lesson to go over that day's material. No grades are given. This is to be a nonthreatening opportunity to review learnings and thoughtfully correct mistakes. The strategy also helps students appreciate that they are learning and making progress. Students typically enjoy Review Tests. (See page 46 for more information on the Review Test strategy.)

Here are two additional strategies that teachers report are effective for wrapping up a class.

Strategy 7.1: Like/Might Review

Description: Students reviewing their recent behavior, noting what they *liked* about it and what they *might* do differently another time.

Purpose: To teach students to review and evaluate their actions constructively and open-mindedly.

First, ask students to think back over what they did or did not do in class and to write some sentences beginning with the phrase "I liked the way I. . . . " Students often write such sentences as:

- I liked the way I spoke up.
- I liked the way I took my time and changed my mind.
- I liked the way I did my outline.

When you see that some students are winding down their writing, say, "Just one more moment, please."

Next tell students to again review their behavior in the class and this time to finish the phrase "Next time I might. . . . " At this point, it's useful to give students one or two examples, such as:

- Next time I might volunteer sooner.
- Next time I might pick an easier topic.
- Next time I might not rush so much.

It's useful also to emphasize that students are to write anything they *might* do differently next time, not something they necessarily *promise* to do next time.

The main intent of this strategy is to give students practice in reviewing their experiences constructively and thoughtfully. The "like" part of the strategy often moves students to notice their talents and better appreciate themselves. The "might" part reminds them that they don't need to repeat past behaviors; they can live and learn, adjusting their behavior wisely.

There's no need for students to share their notes, but you may want to ask them to do so, perhaps using the Whip Around, Pass Option strategy. Or you may ask them to sit in Sharing Pairs and discuss some of what they've written, though I always preface this by telling them they can keep any part private if they wish. Often students like hearing what their classmates have written in a Like/Might Review. Such sharing tends to build an accepting community climate.

Strategy 7.2: Thought/Feel Cards

Description: Notes students make, usually anonymously, of personal thoughts or feelings currently in their awareness.

Purpose: To promote healthful self-awareness. Also, when students share notes, to build respectful group relationships.

This two-part strategy requires 3" x 5" cards or small slips of paper. A teacher might say at the conclusion of the lesson:

> "On one side of the card you just received, note some *thoughts* now in your mind. These may be thoughts about anything. You will not need to share what you write. This is just a chance to look inside yourself and see what thoughts you find there.
> "Now, on the other side, write some *feelings* you find inside yourself. How are you feeling? Again, you will not need to show this to anyone."

Once the class climate is secure enough for students to handle this strategy honestly, it serves several valuable purposes. First, it helps students learn the distinction between a thought and a feeling. Some students are not sure of that distinction. As a result they have difficulty keeping their emotional reactions separate from their reasoning power and thus have special difficulty using their minds to manage their impulses.

This strategy also gives students a chance to vent their feelings and thereby get ready to move ahead to the next lesson with a clear mind. It also suggests that writing is always a safe way to vent one's feelings, in that way teaching a useful life skill.

Thought-Feel Cards also promote self-awareness and self-acceptance. If the strategy is repeated from time to time, perhaps every three or four weeks, students undoubtedly learn something interesting about how their lives are moving along.

After students have completed their card writing, I sometimes ask volunteers to share some of their Thought-Feel notes, perhaps in a whole-class Attentive Discussion, in a Whip Around, Pass Option, or in Sharing Pairs. Other times, I collect the cards, instructing students not to sign their names. I might then shuffle cards and read one side aloud to the class as a kind of feedback about what is happening to the class, taking care not to reveal who wrote anything and not to read something I think might be troublesome to anyone. I may read the cards aloud as soon as I receive them or I may read them aloud the next time the class meets, which gives me time to consider if reading any would further my class purposes. This feedback procedure helps students know they are not alone, not abnormal, not peculiar. They come to see that others in the class share their unspoken thoughts or feelings. Even if I do not read any card aloud, this strategy helps me know how students are responding to my teaching so I can plan for future classes.

A Teacher Comments

I was doing a tutorial when a thunderstorm occurred. The students lost all interest in what we were doing. I took advantage of the situation and had everyone complete a Thought/Feel Card. Then we did a Whip Around. Everyone felt so much better. Several students had been frightened, and the activity helped them see that others felt that way too.

—H. Goldsmith

8 Strategies for Cooperative Group Work

Cooperative group work in the classroom has many advantages. It frees teachers' time and energy so they can spend more time working individually with students. And it makes for productive, active learning. Students who need explanations can often get them more quickly and personally when other students do the explaining, and students who explain ideas to others strengthen their own understanding in the process. Group work also gives students opportunities to participate in a greater variety of experiences: they have many more chances to speak, take initiative, make choices, and generally develop good lifelong learning habits.

Much information on cooperative group learning is available. Experts on this topic include Robert Slavin and Roger and David Johnson. If you want more information on cooperative learning, you may want to consult their writings, some of which are listed in the Recommended Resources for Chapter 8 on page 188.

Determining the Size of Groups

Group size is important to the success of cooperative learning. I believe smaller groups generally work better because they maximize participation by all students. I use pairs whenever possible, so I know that every student is either talking to someone or listening to someone. Pairs readily start and maintain involvement, which is especially valuable considering the short attention span of many of today's students. Pairs are also less noisy than larger groups; two students sitting close together can easily hear each other speak without raising their voices. Pairs also promote good eye contact, which encourages honest communication and helps produce respectful relationships.

I generally avoid forming trios because two of the three students often are more compatible with one another, leaving one student feeling left out. When the class is composed of an odd number of students, however, I use one trio.

Sometimes a pair will have a task they are unable to handle by themselves. When that happens, I instruct the pair to ask another pair for help. I prefer to give that instruction when first organizing groups: "When you are working in groups, always feel free to ask another group for help. I want us all to be friendly and helpful to one another." Students soon learn that whenever they get stuck they can always ask a friend. They need not come to me.

I do not always use pairs. Sometimes more resources are needed than a pair is likely to have available. When a task calls for much creativity or many different perspectives, I usually use groups of three or four—preferably groups of three, to maximize student involvement.

Groups of four are effective for Support Groups (see Strategy 8.5 on p. 109) because they offer the variety of ideas and perspectives that make for good support. The even number of students in the group makes it more likely that comfortable friendships will develop too.

Groups larger than four usually lead to passive participation. Even if discussion time is shared equally, which is rarely the case, most students must remain quiet most of the time. Involvement falls off dramatically.

Determining the Members of Groups

Self-Selection

Asking students to select their own group members is my preferred way of forming groups. My most common instruction is: "Pair up with someone near you. Go." Sometimes, to encourage students to sit with new partners, I'll ask students to pair up with someone they haven't worked with recently.

Self-selection has many advantages. Once students learn how to handle it, groups form quickly and I need be involved only occasionally, as when one person remains without a group. Self-selection also helps students learn how to take initiative in social situations. "We all need to learn how to start relationships," I may say to my class. "Choosing our own group members will give us practice in doing this. Although reaching out to others may feel risky at first, practice will probably make it easier for you."

Self-selection also helps students learn how to react when people reach out to them. I sometimes hear myself saying: "We all need to learn how to react when people ask us to sit with them. In this class, I'd like us to be kind and generous to everyone. Does that mean you must always accept every invitation? No. We also need to learn to say 'No, thank you' when appropriate. When someone says that to you, just invite another person to join you. I think this is a far better way to proceed than worrying why that person turned you down. Please do not say 'No, thank you' too often in this class, however, or some of us may feel that this class isn't really a community of friendly people. It is important to me that all of us here feel that we belong."

Although self-selection is my preferred method of forming groups, it does have its occasional difficulties. Here are some of the most common problems along with some possible solutions:

Problem 1. Everyone keeps choosing the same people for their groups. Cliques are beginning to form.

Solution: Tell the class that you want students to get to know and work with more than just a few other students. Acknowledge the anxiety many people may feel when they are asked to reach out to new people. Perhaps say: "Today please call up your courage and risk asking someone you haven't worked with before to be your partner."

Occasionally you may have to tell some students not to sit with each other again for, say, the next two weeks. Explain that you want all students to get to know and appreciate one another. Don't be too quick to take this action, however; be willing to allow some time for a secure, cooperative class climate to grow. If you invest enough in climate-building strategies, you'll find that students will soon be willing to work with almost anyone. If you rush this process and push students to reach out too early, you'll probably find that you've slowed the growth of a healthy group climate.

Problem 2. Nobody wants to sit with one of the students in your class. You've had to intervene several times to get him into a group.

Solution: Try speaking privately to a few of the more good-natured students, those most likely to be gracious. Tell them you've noticed that all students aren't readily accepted by others when groups are formed. Ask them to go out of their way, please, to look for students who are being left out and to choose them, modeling for the rest of the class the supportive community spirit the class is supposed to be striving for. You may or may not mention the chronically left-out student by name, depending on what you think is best for that student and whether you believe the students you've spoken with can keep the conversation confidential.

Alternatively, you may face the issue honestly with the whole class and then wait a bit for the lone student to find a role in the group: "I've noticed over the last few days that some students are not chosen for groups as quickly as others. Since we want to learn to get along with everyone and be kind to everyone, I would like you all to go out of your way to make sure everyone has a partner. We do not want anyone here to feel left out. I know you like to be with your good friends, but we want everyone to feel that they are a worthwhile part of the class. Please keep on the lookout for classmates needing help or needing partners. Practice reaching out. Let's build a caring, cooperative community here."

Problem 3. Some students react to your calls for goodwill by never refusing anyone. They feel they must always say yes when someone asks to join them.

Solution: Look for an appropriate time to talk to the class about the wisdom of not trying to please all people all the time, about the wisdom of learning how to say no politely and respectfully, about the wisdom of respecting our own need sometimes to help others and sometimes not to: " Don't be afraid sometimes to say 'No, thank you' if you think it best. We all have to maintain our own limits or we will not be very good to anyone for very long. If people tell you 'No, thank you,' respect their right to do so. Don't ask them why they said it and don't fret about it. We all have our own ways. Simply walk over and ask someone else. You would probably not want to be quizzed about why *you* choose what you choose. Let's respect each other's rights here."

Problem 4. A few students keep gossiping and hardly do any work in their groups.

Solution: Don't complain or scold; those tactics will likely be counterproductive. Instead, try doing nothing the first time you notice the behavior. If you notice the behavior a second time, walk to the students and say, without rancor, just as someone responsible for their learning, "I need you to get right down to work." If this simple authority statement does not work, tell the students that because you want everyone to learn in class, you want them to choose other students to work with during the next two weeks. Skip the warning step you may be tempted to issue, such as, "I'll change your groups if you do not settle down to work." Students tend to hear that as a threat, and threats generally produce more trouble.

Problem 5. Slower students sit together and cannot do some of the academic work.

Solution: I sometimes ask these students to pick different partners in the future. Usually I simply remind them to ask other groups for help whenever they feel stuck. The quicker students usually feel honored with such requests for help. I find, too, that the problem tends to vanish as the group climate grows more secure and cooperative. Eventually, slower students do not restrict themselves to choosing just their slower peers as partners. Sometimes, however, slower students are *best* at helping each other, so I do not always discourage such partnerships.

Structured Procedures for Forming Groups

When you want to inject a little variety into the class, you may want to try one of these procedures for forming groups:

1. Pairing Up Within Categories. This procedure involves asking students to pair up with someone who falls into the same category as they do. For instance: "When I say 'Go' I want you to walk around and pair up using the color red as your category. That is, if you are wearing red, I want you to sit with someone who is also wearing red. If you are not wearing red, sit with someone not wearing red. Go."

I've also used these categories: Hair that touches your shoulder and hair that doesn't touch your shoulder; wearing a belt and not wearing a belt. I've also said, "Hold up two fingers if you were born in an even numbered month, one finger if you were born in an odd numbered month. Pair up with someone in the same category."

2. Counting Off. This procedure is an old favorite. Choose the number of people you want in a group and then divide that number into the total number of students in class. The result is the number you want students to count off before beginning the cycle again. For instance, if you want groups of 4 and have 28 students, divide 4 into 28 to get the count-off number of 7. Students count off through the number 7 until everyone has a number. Then the four 1's sit together, the four 2's sit together, and so on.

3. Playing Card Procedure. Use old decks of cards to put together pairs (or as many students as you want in a group). For pairs, make as many card pairs as you need for the class and distribute them randomly around the class. Then ask students to find the person with the card matching their own.

4. Chalkboard Procedure. This procedure is especially useful when students are finishing individual work at different times and need to form small groups immediately after finishing the work. It involves asking students to write their names on the board as they finish their work. To illustrate, here is a teacher instructing the class on how to form trios: "When you finish your individual work and are ready to work in a trio, write your name on the left side of the chalkboard. If someone has already written a name, write your name under it and then go sit with that person. If two names are already there, erase both names and then go sit with those two people and begin your trio work. The next person would, of course, see no names and write his or her name to begin a new trio group."

Mixed Ability Grouping and Grading

Some teachers prefer forming groups themselves, so they can mix student ability within each group or at least place some high-achieving students in every group. And some teachers prefer to connect students' grades to group work to motivate students to work harder. I find both practices unnecessary. Concerning grades, a combination of quick pace, small group size, and appropriate task assignments eventually motivates students to get involved and stay involved quite as well as—and usually better than—rewards and punishments, and this approach produces far fewer difficulties for me. Deliberately mixing abilities takes too much time away from instruction for me and denies students the learning experiences that come from selecting their own partners.

Strategies for Effective Cooperative Grouping

I have already described two of the most useful cooperative learning strategies in Chapter 2, "Basic Instructional Strategies." These two strategies are:

Underexplain with Learning Pairs. Explain material fairly briefly so that only some students fully understand and then ask students to sit in pairs to help each other fill in the gaps and exchange and deepen understandings.

Sharing Pairs. For example, ask students to turn to a partner and share their opinions on a specific topic, or what they did for homework, or what they wrote down during a Speak-Write Lecture, or their reactions to a whole-class discussion, or the outcome sentences they've written that day, and so on.

Although these two strategies fall under the definition of cooperative learning strategies, they are such a basic part of the teaching approach I advocate that I thought they should be described fully in the chapter on basic instructional strategies. See page 27 for the complete explanation of the Underexplain with Learning Pairs strategy and page 32 for the Sharing Pairs strategy.

Strategy 8.1: Paired Reading

Description: Pairs of students take turns reading aloud to each other.

Purpose: To give students as much practice as possible in oral reading.

This strategy is straightforward. Simply ask students to pair up with someone and to take turns reading aloud a selection you have assigned. You might mention that if they come across something that's hard for them to read, they could ask their partner for help.

Students usually enjoy paired reading. It is much more engaging than what is sometimes called round-robin reading, when one person in a whole class reads aloud and others are asked to follow along until it's their turn to read. Students do not usually tune out during Paired Reading, for they are either reading or staying ready for their reading turn. Paired Reading can be used with almost any reading material, fiction or nonfiction.

I prefer to give minimum directions when I use Paired Reading, partly to allow for maximum self-direction and partly to allow for individual variation in talent. I find students usually know when, for example, to give the reading turn to their partner and how to assist a partner who needs help. When someone asks, "How long should we each read?" I might say, "You choose. You do not have to read the same amount. Read for an amount of time that feels comfortable and fair to both of you."

I usually do give directions for what students are to do when they have completed the reading. For instance:

• Talk over the reading and see what you think about it.
• Each person write in your journal some outcome sentences based on the reading.
• Talk about some things you liked or found interesting. Each of you be ready to report at least one thing.
• If you finish before I call time, you can begin the next reading or shift to some of your individual work.

Although Paired Reading is most often used in elementary schools, some high school teachers report that it's an effective way to inject variety into the class and give special attention to selected text.

Strategy 8.2: Task Group, Share Group

Description: Students considering a problem in small task groups and then regrouping so each student can share task-group work with students who were in different task groups.

Purpose: To maintain high student involvement in group work.

This is a highly involving, flexible small-group activity that I learned initially from Hanoch McCarty of Hanoch McCarty Associates, an education training firm in Galt, California. It proceeds in two steps.

Step 1: Task Group. Assign a group task, for instance:

• Make interesting sentences out of vocabulary words (or spelling words).

• Come up with three or four real-life applications of a multiplication fact, a science idea, or any general principle.

• Write in order of importance to you the government agencies we studied.

• Think of three or more alternatives for handling a real-life problem.

• Write what you think is interesting about . . . (Lincoln, the United Nations, rivers, and so on).

Specify a time frame for the task. Shorter is better than longer because a short time frame encourages students to start promptly and move smartly. Also assign a group size. Smaller is better than larger, and pairs work best; the smaller the group, the larger the active role of each student. Inform students that when time is up, they will pair off with someone not in their task group to share a few of their group's ideas, so they might make notes, if they like, to be ready for that sharing.

Step 2: Share Group. When the time for Step 1 is up, instruct students to find one person not in their working group, to sit with that person, and then to take turns sharing some of their groups' ideas. With task groups of two, you might say, "Okay, pairs. Identify one person in your pair as 'A' and the other as 'B.' Ready? Now I'd like the A's to remain seated. B's, please stand and find a new 'A' to be your partner. B's will then share with your new partner something about what you did or learned in your task group. Then, A's, you take a turn and share what your task group did or learned. We don't have much time for this, so move quickly. Go!" I recommend, as usual, a fairly quick pace. For high-level involvement and learning, sharing sessions are usually best kept short.

A second or third set of sharing pairs is sometimes useful, as when a variety of important learnings is involved, or when quiet students could use more experience in speaking to peers. For extra sharing, when time is up simply say, "Now, please find another partner and share either what you did in your task group or, if you like, some ideas that came up in your first sharing pair." A whole-class discussion might follow, or students could write personal outcome sentences, perhaps for a large-group Whip Around, Pass Option activity or for inclusion in individual portfolios.

Some teachers prefer to give task groups a choice of problems. To set the stage for this, for instance, a teacher says to students, "We talked about China. What ideas from China might be useful for us here in the United States? We might wonder, for example, if a typical American family might be able to learn something about family life from a typical Chinese family. Let's see if we can list other possibly useful ideas from China." The teacher writes students' responses on the board and then says, "Please get a partner and sit in pairs. Each pair pick one issue listed on the board, one that you are both interested in. Then talk about the advantages and disadvantages of people in our country learning something from the Chinese about that. If your pair picked 'family life' as your issue, for instance, consider some things we might learn that would affect family life in the United States in both positive and negative ways. Later we'll sit in new pairs so you can hear what other groups talked about."

A Teacher Comments

Students love to hear me read them stories. And I enjoy it too. But lately I often use Task Group, Share Groups. I ask students to pair up and take turns reading parts of a story to each other. "No one read too long," I say, "so both have turns. But please read at least one sentence. Ask your partner for help with a word, if you like, or just guess. When you are done, take turns giving answers to the questions on this poster: What happened so far? What do you predict might happen next? Any predictions on how the story might end? Have you any reasons for your prediction?"

For Step 2 of the process, I tell students, "When I say Go, find a new partner. Take turns telling what you or your task partner think might happen. Just two minutes for this. Go." Somehow students really get up for this reading activity.

—Miriam Harmon, 2nd grade teacher

Strategy 8.3: Option Display

Description: Small groups work on a problem, aiming to construct a display that shows several options for solving the problem, the likely consequences of each option, and the group's best overall recommendation.

Purpose: To teach students how to attack problems open-mindedly and thoughtfully.

---

1. Develop a Problem. The Option Display strategy begins with the development of an open-ended problem, such as one of the following:

• *In language arts:* (1) How can we help the young students in our school who cannot read well? (2) How can we best distribute the magazine the class produced? (3) How can violence on television be reduced?

• *In math:* (1) How can we remember all the geometry formulas? (2) How can we keep track of the cost of a cart of groceries? (3) How can we estimate the number of beans in a bottle?

• *In social studies:* (1) What might reduce prejudice in this country? (2) How might we help the people who are living in poverty in our area? (3) How might we get more people voting in elections?

• *In science/health:* (1) How can we measure temperature without a thermometer? (2) How can we provide better health care to infants? (3) How can we better dispose of all our garbage?

Problems may call for research or creative thinking, and you may assign the problem to the class or allow students to select a problem from a short list.

2. Form Small Groups. Once a problem has been selected, the class breaks into small groups. Pairs usually work best. Larger groups have more ideas, but they also result in more passive participation. If everyone is working on the same problem, groups may be formed in any way you find convenient. If students were offered more than one problem to choose from, students who have selected the same problem could form groups. Alternatively, groups could form first and then jointly choose a problem.

3. Explain the Option Display. Explain that students are to produce (by an agreed upon time) a wall chart containing four elements:

• On the top of the chart, a clear *statement of the problem,* in their own words.

• On the left side of the chart, a list of three or more possible *options for handling the problem.* This should include as many reasonable ideas as students can identify by reading, thinking, or interviewing people.

• On the right side, next to each option, the chief *advantages and disadvantages* of each option. Students should think ahead to the difficulties and benefits that would likely result if that option were carried out. They should think ahead to long-term consequences.

• On the bottom of the chart, the team's *overall recommendation.* What does the team think would be the best way to handle the problem?

Tell students they must sign their names on the completed chart. Also tell them that the charts will be displayed for some time, so all will have a chance to examine their group's ideas.

4. Review and Conclusion. Post the option display charts long enough for students to review them. Then perhaps ask students questions like these:

• Did anyone get any new ideas from this activity?

• Did anyone change their mind about something because of the activity?

• What do you think is the best solution to this problem?

• Does the activity suggest steps you might take when you face a tough problem in your life?

Strategy 8.4: Best Choice Debate

Description: Pairs of students first prepare either a pro or con position on a controversial issue. A pro pair and a con pair then join to (1) explain their position to each other and (2) seek agreement on the quartet's best overall recommendation.

Purpose: To help students learn how to research a controversial issue and share thoughts open-mindedly.

Debates can be viewed in two ways: as contests with winners and losers or as structured discussions designed to consider two opposing arguments. The first approach leads to antagonism and distortion of information. The second approach is much more constructive, similar to Johnson and Johnson's (1987) "constructive controversy." Best Choice Debates might focus on such controversial questions as these:

- Should possibly harmful fertilizers be outlawed?
- Should property and sales taxes be replaced by income taxes?
- Should children have an evening curfew?
- Should music with vulgar language be limited?
- Should the minimum driving age be lowered?
- Should we require everyone to use the metric system?
- Should children get an allowance?
- Should handguns be outlawed?
- Should the workweek be limited to 20 hours so more people could find jobs?

Here is an example of how a teacher might initially use the Best Choice Debate strategy with students. The question under consideration is: "Should smoking be illegal?"

"I would like you to form pairs for this next activity. Please pair up with someone with whom you have not worked recently. I will arbitrarily assign half the pairs to take the Yes side of our question: You will perhaps need to pretend it, but your position is that you strongly agree that smoking should be illegal. Half the pairs will be assigned the No position: You will strongly disagree that smoking should be illegal.

"The procedure has three main steps. The first is *preparation time*. This is where you will work with your partner to understand your side of the issue. Please be able to clearly state your reasons and have evidence to support your opinion so that you are well prepared to face an opposing pair later.

"The second step is *debate time*. At this step, I will then put two opposing pairs together so you will face two students who are prepared to argue the opposing position. Your job is twofold. First, partners cooperate to get the other pair to fully appreciate your position. At the outset, they may not understand it at all. In fact, since they were preparing the other side of the issue, they may be committed to their side and have trouble listening to your reasons with an open mind. You will need, then, to practice a skill often useful throughout life—getting people who think differently from you to understand your viewpoint. Note that your goal is not to convince the other pair that they are wrong and you are right. Your goal, as a pair, is to make sure they understand your side of the issue.

"The second part of your task is to pretend you do not now understand their position. If you did not do this, they would have no practice in communicating effectively, which is the first task. This does not mean you have to be stubborn or argumentative. Don't go to extremes. This is not a beat-the-opposition debate. It's really a search for expanded, balanced understandings. So even if you fully understand the thinking of the other pair, pretend you do not. If you think it will not be too upsetting, you can even show some disagreement with their ideas, so they can practice communicating with people who openly disagree with them. At some time in life, you will all probably have to deal with people who think differently from you, so now is a good time to practice.

"The third step in this activity is called *best choice time*. At this step, I will ask each quartet to see if they can agree on the best choice for resolving the issue. In other words, now that the four of you understand more about both sides of the issue, what do you think, overall, is best for all concerned? Make smoking illegal? Leave the law as it stands? Or perhaps your group can come up with a third choice. We do not want to get stuck in either-or thinking. We will just use this debate strategy to open up our discussions.

"One hint before we begin preparation time: During the quartet discussions, you may face problems. What do you do, for example, if you and your partner do not cooperate very well, and even contradict each other, making it hard for the other pair to understand your position? What do you do if an argument breaks out and people stop listening to each other? These and other problems might emerge. It would be smart to use some of your preparation time to talk about how you will handle such problems. Do you want to talk now about options for handling the two problems I just mentioned? Do you want to identify other problems that might come up before we form pairs, assign positions, and get into our planning time?"

After a discussion of how to handle problems, students form groups and proceed with the debate. Sometimes I will interject a lecture at some point in the activity, to ensure that students are familiar with the more subtle points in the issue. I usually do this after the initial pairs have begun to work but before they have completed their preparations.

After the third step, I often use a whole-class Attentive Discussion, which I focus both on the issue under discussion and, later, on the experiences students had in cooperating and explaining. As a wrap-up,

I usually call for individual outcome sentences, inviting statements about both the issue discussed and the process of cooperating and explaining. I typically conclude by asking each student to share one or two outcome sentences in a whole-class Whip Around, Pass Option activity.

Strategy 8.5: Support Group

Description: Several students, usually a group of four, who regularly sit together and offer appropriate support to one another.

Purpose: To ensure that all students feel they belong and have access to peer support.

A support group is composed of several students who sit together every day for the express purpose of offering one another continual support. I find groups of four work best. Group members may exchange phone numbers and help one another other when they have questions about homework or need to catch up when they are absent from class. Support group members may also read one another's portfolios and suggest improvements. They may share personal problems and talk through solutions. Each group may also have a class task to complete, such as taking attendance or passing out books. In addition, one person in each group may be responsible for, say, collecting support group papers for the teacher, handling group lunch money, or marking absences for group members.

In general, group members are asked to sit together in class and to support one another in whatever ways they believe are appropriate. The groups may remain stable for several weeks or even half a year. Such groups often help the class develop a strong class climate of community.

I generally recommend forming groups by some random method, so students learn to get along with all sorts of people. Before disbanding and forming new groups, I like to ask students to exchange "I Appreciate" messages:

> "Write your name on a card and pass it to the other members of your support group. When you get a card, write one or more things you honestly appreciate about that person—what he or she once said or did or wore . . . anything at all, anything you can say that you honestly appreciate about the person. Then

each of you keep your cards, and anytime you feel low, you can pull them out and remind yourself that other people really do appreciate you."

Although Support Groups may also be used for instructional purposes, I prefer to focus their attention on other matters, such as keeping up with routines, building friendships, and generally getting along. I treat Support Groups rather like family groups, a stable home base within a class community. For instructional purposes, I recommend using Learning Pairs, Sharing Pairs, Task Groups, and the like.

Strategy 8.6: Project Work

Description: Students working on a task for an extended time period, alone or in small groups, usually to produce a tangible product.

Purpose: To help students become more responsible learners and to motivate students to work cooperatively and intelligently.

Some classrooms thrive on a steady diet of relatively complex student projects. If you are unpracticed at using such project work in your classroom, you will probably need to experiment to find ways to make projects work smoothly for you. The hardest part is often giving up control, trusting students to grow into the challenges. The best part is usually seeing students become energetic and responsible as they work on the projects. Let's look at how to get started.

Project Options

Projects need some kind of focus. It may be a subject matter concept, such as plant growth, world government, weights and measures, sonnets, or harmony. Or it may be an interdisciplinary theme, such as designing an ideal city, graphing the answers to interview questions, considering the health of senior citizens and developing a program to help improve it, or studying kite building. I recommend that projects be done in study teams, as described by the teacher in the following example:

"Our next unit is on rivers. I thought we could have one group studying the formation of rivers: How do they start? Where do they start? What is necessary for a river to continue to flow over many centuries? Another group could study the local river: What can we discover by studying it? A third group might identify the major rivers of the world and their characteristics. A fourth group could investigate rivers as a means of transportation. There are other ways to approach rivers: Their contribution to the economy, the way they have been used by artists and writers, their connection to issues of ecology, the fish and plant life commonly found in and around them them. What other focus could a study team take?"

You can help students get projects off the ground by encouraging a class to brainstorm a list of what they already know about the topic followed by a list of what they might want to know (see Strategy 14.4 on page 178). The brainstorming can lead into a group discussion of how they might organize their project groups.

Teams can be organized around an *action project*, the focus of which is taking action rather than studying; for instance the project may be producing a monthly class magazine:

"Everyone can contribute writing and artwork. You can use parts of your journals, even your doodles. But we need groups to put the magazine together and get it out. We might, for instance, have a typing team. And a proofreading team. And a team that takes care of the duplication. Another, say, for publicity and distribution. Or collecting material from parents and other classes, if we want that. I think we'll need people to manage the fund-raising. They could also take care of the bookkeeping. Each of you can be on more than one team, of course. And maybe we'll need other teams. What do you think?"

Here are some other possible action projects:

• Carrying out a tutoring program for younger students in the school.

• Investigating alternative remedies for an existing problem in the cafeteria or community.

• Managing a program for finding adults willing to consult in the class or accept students as temporary apprentices.

• Conducting public opinion polls on issues of interest to each group.

• Talking to recognized experts in various fields and getting their opinions on drugs, health care, crime prevention, family values, and so on.

• Constructing a greenhouse for school use.

• Creating exhibits showing space exploration in the past and future.

• Designing and preparing a model of the ideal home, car, or city.

• Preparing an assembly for the school.

Projects may be based on *student interests*:

> "We will cover many important topics in our class, but I would really like you to practice learning on your own, perhaps to become more skillful in an area that interests you or to learn more about a topic. You could work at this 'personal project,' as I call it, alone or with one or two others. If you work with others, I want to keep the groups small, pairs or trios at the most, so all of you have important parts to play in your groups. Most of the time you will need to work outside class. But you can probably substitute personal project work for some class work. Speak to me if you think such a substitution would serve your best interests."
>
> "What should your project focus on? Almost anything you think would be fun or good for you. Overcoming procrastination, perhaps. The history of bicycles. Chess. Secret codes. Mark Twain. Labor unions. Heroines in history. Scuba diving requirements. Computer art. The concept of generosity, or imagination, or pantomime, or discrimination. Modern music. Improving your sleep habits. Perhaps improving your staying-awake habits. In short, almost anything you are serious about pursuing. Just check with me before you start. I'll ask you to draw up a tentative plan of action and turn in, say, weekly progress cards. Then we'll go from there."

Guidelines for Project Work

• **Clear time lines.** Specific deadlines are essential. Give students reasonable time to complete project tasks but don't make the mistake of allowing too much time, because many students will then develop the habit of dawdling over their work. Reasonable time limits keep students on task.

• **Progress reports.** For projects requiring work over an extended time, progress reports are valuable. You might request a weekly report of what the students have accomplished and what specific plans the students have for the following week. Each student could submit this information every Friday or group members could rotate the job of reporting for the group.

• **Final product.** Students should understand what the final product of their project work is to be. The final product could be any number of things. For instance, it could be a collaborative written report, personal outcome sentences, personal notes that each student will use to report on their group's work to a student from a different project group (as in the Task Group, Share Group strategy), a chart showing the group's ideas (as in the Option Display strategy) together with any "minority" viewpoints. I do not recommend that students prepare a series of oral reports for the class as a whole unless the reports are particularly creative; oral reports tend quickly to bore many students. (See the Creative Reports strategy in Chapter 12 on page 159 for more suggestions.)

• **Avoid copy work.** Avoid projects that involve routine copy work from a text or encyclopedia. Rather than ask students to simply report on crime prevention, for example, ask them to "summarize the opinions of three experts and interview at least five adults to see what they think of that expert advice." Or ask them to "design an ideal health center, including a nutrition program and illness prevention help." Assigning students specific tasks like these helps reduce copy work:

• Interview.
• Compare opinions.
• Make a model.
• Design an ideal _____.
• Find contrasting views on _____.
• Produce a mural.
• Prepare an educational debate.
• Create a dramatic presentation for another class.

On Project Power

As many teachers have long known, student projects offer unique advantages. No other strategy is nearly as effective in developing students' self-management skills. Nor is any as likely to make subject matter learning as personally meaningful to students. Projects are also unsurpassed in helping students learn about life in general, including lifelong study skills and skills for getting along with others. In addition, student project work frees teachers from many routine chores and gives students the opportunity to exhibit high dignity, energy, self-management, community, and awareness.

Strategy 8.7: Task and Team Skill Group ───────

Description: A small group of students working at a task and simultaneously practicing an interpersonal skill.

Purpose: To develop students' teamwork skills.

───

This strategy, adapted from *A Guidebook for Cooperative Learning* by Dee Dishon and Pat Wilson O'Leary (1984), is a powerful form of cooperative learning. It advances not only academic learning but effective interpersonal skills. The strategy takes some time, however—usually a minimum of 45 minutes. Four steps are involved:

Step 1: Assign an individual task. The individual task may simply be assigned as homework. For instance, each student could be asked to:

- Identify four or more new ideas from a text.
- Collect examples of a specific physics principle.
- Write down some personal recommendations for preventing waste in school.
- Write a poem.
- Draft a letter to the editor on an issue the student feels strongly about.
- Seek real-life applications for a math procedure.

Step 2: Assign a group product. The product should build on the above individual tasks while giving students the opportunity to practice a teamwork skill. Students work together in groups of two to four to produce this specific, tangible product to be signed by all persons in the group. Here are some examples of products that might be assigned for the individual tasks listed above:

- A list of ideas from the text ranked by importance.
- A report of physics examples synthesized and augmented by any new ideas that arose during the group interaction.
- A list of individual ideas for preventing waste ranked by estimated long-term effectiveness.
- An illustrated book of poems.
- An improved version of the original draft letters to the editor.
- A poster showing a real-life math problem with a clear, illustrated solution on an attached sheet.

In using this strategy, be sure to tell students that they are to practice one or two specific teamwork skills while they are working in their groups. Here are some examples of skills you might specify:

- listening closely to each person
- taking turns
- returning to the task when they notice they are off it
- disagreeing politely
- managing time
- asking for help
- being supportive
- sharing honest feelings
- keeping all involved
- paraphrasing
- helping without giving answers
- expressing honest appreciation
- listening with empathy
- disciplining unproductive impulses
- making everyone feel important
- making eye contact.

It's best to define the assigned teamwork skill with many examples, so students have specific guidance when practicing it. To illustrate, here is a teacher providing this kind of guidance for her class:

> "While doing this task, I'd like you to focus on being supportive of one another. Let's brainstorm some things a person might do or say that would suggest the person is being supportive. And let's also brainstorm some things a person might say or do that might be not supportive at all." The class then brainstorms and produces some ideas: supportive people nod, smile, thank others, give credit to others; unsupportive people do not listen, look out the window, don't help, are slow to join in discussions.

You may want to invite students to select specific roles for their group work: group coordinator, time watcher, recorder, keeper of materials, and so on. I usually do not recommend role assignments, however; I prefer to keep groups small enough so that all group members quite naturally have important roles to play.

At this point, also tell students how much time they have to produce the assigned product and practice the assigned skill. It's best if no penalty is given to groups that fail to complete the task, because the threat of penalties can add excessive anxiety to the task. Besides, this kind of task can usually be made interesting enough to motivate students' natural interest in being involved.

Step 3: Review the teamwork skill. It's usually best to review the teamwork skill as soon as groups have produced their products, while the experience is fresh, with the aim of helping students clarify what they learned about that skill.

One effective review procedure starts with students making notes. Ask students to think back over the group time and note what they *liked* about what they or someone in their group did with the skill being practiced. Then ask students to note what they *might* do next time they have a chance to practice this skill. Next ask students to note some other places in their lives, perhaps with friends or families, they would like to see people better using the skill. Finally, invite a few students to share something they've noted. This sharing usually leads to a productive five- or ten-minute discussion.

Step 4. Review the task. The final step is to review the task with the aim of advancing students' understanding of the subject matter. Here are some possible ways to proceed:

• Lecture on the task and then draw out understandings from the group in an Attentive Discussion.

• Ask students to post the results of their task groups and then have everyone walk around and read over one another's work, either during that class period or at some time in the near future.

• Ask students to pair up with someone not in their task group and share their experiences.

• Ask students to write outcome sentences about the subject matter and then share those in a discussion or a Whip Around.

Strategy 8.8: Hand-Raising Signal

Description: The teacher raises a hand to signal the end of small-group discussion; students who see the hand then raise their own hand. Hands stay raised until all discussion has ceased.

Purpose: To quickly and easily get the attention of students who are working in groups.

Sometimes you want quickly to get students' attention while they are working in groups. The Hand-Raising Signal is an easy way to do this. Here's one way it might be explained to a class:

> "When I raise my hand during small-group time, I'm signaling that it's time to stop your discussion. When you see my hand go up, please raise your hand. When you raise your hand, people who cannot see me will see hands go up and raise their hands. If you are talking when hands go up, please finish the sentence you have started, but do not start a new sentence.
>
> "If you were saying or doing something important before I gave this signal, which will sometimes happen, please remember what it was. I may be asking you to stop your discussion because I need to give you new directions or because I want you to speak more quietly. Sometimes I'll tell you to continue your group discussion, other times I'll tell you we're moving on to a new activity. If we do move on, please remember that you can always continue your discussion at lunch or after school."

The Hand-Raising signal is especially valuable for quieting a noisy class. I suspect it works so well because it gives all students something to do—raise their hands—and does not focus on what a few students should stop doing—talking. The strategy is active and constructive. It can even be adapted to nonclassroom settings, as Clara Bowles, a 3rd grade teacher, reports:

> I use the Hand-Raising Signal on the playground. When I need students to come inside, I raise my hand. Students who see me raise theirs and soon all the hands are in the air. The students somehow enjoy going through the process and I do not have to yell or complain. They just do it and I wave them in. It works wonderfully well.

9

Strategies for Efficiently Using Class Time

Teaching an enormous amount of subject matter to a variety of students over several months is a job requiring a master organizer. It involves managing time, materials, and the pressures and expectations that others pile on us—and that we occasionally pile on ourselves. Other chapters of this book contain strategies for handling particular aspects of this complex job, while this chapter contains seven generally valuable strategies for using our time efficiently.

Strategy 9.1: Intelligence Call Up

Description: Reminders that inspire students to call up and exercise their natural human intelligence.

Purpose: To advance students' ability to handle their lives responsibly, wisely.

Grace Pilon, developer of WORKSHOP WAY®, taught me the value of repeatedly telling students they are smart enough to solve problems on their own. To see how the Intelligence Call Up strategy works, let's look at a 1st grade teacher announcing thoughtful problem solving as the norm in her classroom:

> "When things are not flowing smoothly in this class, I want you to pause and ask yourself, "What would be the smart, intelligent thing to do?" So, for example, if papers are not being

piled neatly, or a crowd is forming at the door, I might say to you, 'What would be the smart, thoughtful way to handle this situation? Stop and think about this for a minute, and then go ahead and do what you think would be best.'

"Let's use our brains. We want this to be a class in which we all learn how to think for ourselves. Let's develop our intelligence. From time to time, I'll remind you that we're trying to do that.

"If you were not a human with a human brain, you might not know what is best to do. But you have an amazing brain. You can think for yourself. When things are not going right, call up your intelligence. Pause and ask yourself, 'What is the smart thing to do now?' Learn to reason things out for yourself. Humans can do that like no other animal.

"Can anyone give an example of when something was not going smoothly, and you stopped and thought about what was best to do, or maybe what you had to stop doing, and you did that?"

Here are some incidents that illustrate how an 8th grade teacher used the Intelligence Call Up strategy:

• **Students fail to clean up on time.** "Class, we're having difficulty getting everything cleaned up on time. How can we handle this problem? Let's brainstorm a list of ideas on the board. We are smart enough to find a way to solve this problem that will be good for us all. After the brainstorming, we'll see what we think is best."

• **When asked to form pairs, some students repeatedly form the same pairs and avoid certain students.** "Class, I'm having to use extra time to pair up everyone when I call for Sharing Pairs. I can understand that you want to sit with your good friends. But getting everyone involved is taking us too much time. Besides, I want us to learn to get along with everyone here. From now on, pair up with someone you haven't worked with before or haven't worked with in quite a while. You're smart; you'll know whom you've worked with and whom you haven't worked with. And please make sure everyone gets a partner quickly, that nobody feels left out."

• **Preparing a class for the arrival of new students.** "Here's a chance to exercise our brain power. We will get new students from time to time. What's the best way to get them into the flow of our work? We could discuss this question now and use our creativity all together. Or would it be better to ask a committee to think it through and give us a recommendation or two? What do you think is best?"

• **A student asks a question about an important but not absolutely vital issue.** "You decide," the teacher says in a tone that conveys the message *I trust you to exercise your self-management abilities wisely.*

• **Two students come to the teacher complaining about each other.** "Talk it over. If necessary, write down your options. Then work it out yourselves. Use your creative intelligence. Work it out together."

In short, the Intelligence Call Up strategy lets students know that the teacher expects intelligent behavior from them, and that the teacher trusts students to make intelligent decisions. It transfers a teacher's high expectations for intelligent behavior to students and eventually makes intelligent behavior second nature to students.

Assuring Students That They *Are* Intelligent

Some students do not believe they are intelligent. Perhaps parents confused grades with intelligence or compared one child with another, or perhaps earlier class experiences did not fit the students' learning styles. Many experiences may have led students to discount their ability to think and live intelligently. To overcome such negative impressions, you may want to assure students that all humans have a remarkable intelligence. Continued use of the Intelligence Call Up strategy is an excellent way to do that. You may also want to find a way to discuss intelligence with students, especially to help them distinguish human brain power from school grades. I like to do this by telling students about my father, who never went to high school and never did much reading, but was one of the smartest people I've ever known. He knew what was going on, and he knew what would likely happen next.

After telling the class about my father, I say, "What does it mean to be intelligent? It is certainly not a matter of being able to remember facts or solve school problems. Some of you can do that better than others. But *all* humans can do much more. All humans are aware. And all humans can manage that awareness. Look at that window. Now look at the ceiling. That is managing your awareness. You are directing your attention where you want it. All humans can do that. When you think about what to do next, you are simply managing your awareness, focusing your awareness on the options ahead. Being intelligent is nothing more than that: directing your awareness where you want it.

The better you can manage awareness, and the more things you can bring into awareness, the more powerful your intelligence will be.

"I encourage you to practice using that intelligence. Reach to become more aware of what is going on around you and inside you, including inside your head where, if you are patient enough, you will find lots of good ideas. And including the world around you where, if you listen and observe closely, you will notice many interesting events.

"And reach to become better at managing that awareness, focusing it for longer periods on one thing, looking more closely at details and looking more widely at the general scene. Practice that and you will learn how to use more of your native intelligence.

"When you're unsure of what is best to do, pause and become more aware of what is going on. Then reach for all the ideas you can dream up. Perhaps ask others for ideas, too. As our sign says, it's intelligent to ask for help. After you get ideas about what can be done, imagine what will happen when you choose to do one thing or another. That's what it means to think ahead. Think like that and you'll be exercising your natural smartness. Thinking ahead will help you to live an intelligent life, like my father did."

Strategy 9.2: Set of Speakers

Description: Requesting volunteers to speak and then, from all volunteers, choosing a set of students who will have a turn.

Purpose: To efficiently select speakers.

Rather than call on one student at a time during discussions, occasionally select a set of students. "How many would be willing to share ideas?" you might ask. Hands go up and you point to some: "Let's hear from five people today. You be first. You be second . . . " After you've selected the set, say, "Let's hear now from the first person." The remaining speakers know their turns are coming up and they know the order in which they will speak. The rest of the class knows the next bit of time is all organized and they need not worry about whether to speak, so they can pay more careful attention to the discussion that follows.

Choosing a set of students also makes it easier to avoid repeatedly calling on the same students and easier to notice the more tentative hands almost ready to be raised. I sometimes prompt more volunteers with something like, "How about some new volunteers?" Or, "Katanya, I see you might be willing to be a speaker. How about volunteering?"

I also like to use the Whip Around, Pass Option strategy, sometimes down one row, sometimes around the whole class. That strategy usually produces widespread participation, assuming I have built a cooperative class atmosphere, an atmosphere that respects risk taking and the truth of the sign *It's okay to make mistakes. That's the way we learn.*

Strategy 9.3: Nod of Recognition

Description: A nod to a student that indicates the teacher is aware the student has volunteered.

Purpose: To allow time for more students to volunteer.

Usually a few bright students quickly volunteer to answer questions. To avoid calling on those few students all the time, you might explain to the class that you'll be using the nod of recognition: "Sometimes I'll ask for volunteers to answer a question, you will raise your hand, and I will not call on you or anyone else for a moment or two. I might just look at you and nod. That means I noticed you were willing to volunteer, so you can put down your hand. I simply want to wait a bit before calling on anyone, to give more time for people to think about the question and to consider whether they are willing to risk giving an answer." When I use this strategy in my classroom, students seem to understand my motive and respect it.

Strategy 9.4: Once Principle

Description: Announcing that directions will be given only once and that students needing help are to use their intelligence and find an appropriate way to catch up.

Purpose: To teach students both to listen and live responsibly.

Imagine a teacher saying the following: "Please, everyone, look at me. From now on, I will say things only once. Page numbers. Directions. Anything like that. So please practice keeping yourself aware. If you miss what I say, find a way to catch up. Perhaps whisper to a friend or watch and see what others are doing or later catch what you missed.

Call on your good intelligence. You will know the best thing to do. Now let's get started on today's lesson." The teacher says this only once. He does not ask "Any questions?" because that might lead to a repetition of the message. And note that the teacher begins by asking all students to look at him. If a direction is to be given only once, it is imperative to call for attention and leave an appropriate beat of silence to avoid the confusion that would undoubtedly result from directions given in a noisy room. It is only fair to call for attention so all students have a chance to hear the directions.

Will all procedures work if teachers say things only once? Yes, they will. When students realize that asking the teacher to repeat due dates or page numbers for assignments will produce only a smile from the teacher, not even an "I *told* you," or "I say things only once" or "Please check with a neighbor," students will learn to manage just fine, because they are far from stupid. If we expect students to abide by the Once Principle, they will. In my experience, it is more difficult for teachers to stick with the Once Principle than for students to change their behavior in response to it.

Strategy 9.5: Class Tutors

Description: Students who are ready to tutor classmates needing extra help.

Purpose: To provide students who need extra help an easy and efficient means of getting it.

I find great advantage in peer teaching. It usually helps both the giver and the receiver, not only with learning subject matter but in developing habits that will serve students for a lifetime. Here's an example of how you might introduce peer tutoring to your class:

> "We all learn by our own time clocks and in our own ways, of course. Some of us learn things slower, some faster. That's not good or bad; it's just another example of how we're all different. Our differences make us more able to help one another see things in new ways. In our class, I want us to do that. I want us to live as a cooperative, kind community. One way each of you can contribute is by volunteering to be class tutors on selected topics. A class tutor is someone who understands a topic well and is willing to help others understand it better. Those of you

who understand a topic and are willing to be class tutors on that topic, please sign the topic sheet I have posted in the tutor section over there. Then, when someone would like some help, they can look on that sheet and find someone to ask for help.

"Notice that the sign-up sheet asks whether you are willing to help someone after school and during the school day. You might do your tutoring on the phone, if you and the person you are tutoring agree that this is okay.

"I might also use the tutor list. If I notice a few students whom I want to get extra help or practice, I might use the list to see what tutors I could place the students with. If I ever do that, I will tell the tutor exactly what it is that I want covered in the tutoring session."

Of course, most students will need some training if they are to be good class tutors. Strategy 9.6 can help you provide the proper training.

Strategy 9.6: Tutor Training

Description: Lessons teaching students skills for effectively giving and receiving help.

Purpose: To teach basic communication skills.

I recommend training all students to be tutors in part because the skills used in tutoring are also used in ordinary group work. Tutor training also gives us a perfect opportunity to teach important life skills, such as how to listen to others, how to discipline urges to upstage others, and how to converse productively with others. When students receive training in tutoring, they are usually better able to both give and receive help.

Here's a three-step process for tutor training in the junior high grades:

Step 1: Practice Pairs

Whole class
1 minute

"I will sometimes ask you to help one another with your learning, usually by working in pairs. Some of you may also volunteer to be tutors for certain topics. But what does it take to help someone learn? I think you will find that, first off, it takes good listening by the tutors. In most situations, you have to listen to people to be able to determine the best way to help them."

Whole class brainstorming
4–12 minutes

"How many of you know someone who listens really well? Does anyone know someone who is a terrible listener? Let's consider what good listeners do that terrible listeners do not do. Sam and Jean, will you write our ideas on the board as we think of them?"

Instructions and Practice pairs
4 minutes

"Here are three key skills of good listeners: (1) they look at you pleasantly (not look out the window) while you talk, (2) they give you plenty of time to think, and (3) they don't interrupt. When I give the signal, I want you to find a new partner, someone you haven't work with recently. One of you will be *A* and the other, *B*. *A* will start. *A*'s job is to talk about someone who is either a fairly good listener or a very poor listener. *B*'s job is to be a good listener. I'll signal when 90 seconds is up. Until then, *B*, do not take the focus from *A*. You'll have a turn later. Get in pairs now and begin."

Whole-class discussion
2–5 minutes

"How many *A*'s had *B*'s who did a super job listening, even though this was the first time we tried this? What problems came up? What did you all learn from this?"

Second instructions and practice
4 minutes

"Let's reverse roles now. *B*'s, you talk about listening, your experience just now, people you know, anything. *A*'s, check the three key listening skills. Your job is not to steal the focus from *B*, to be as good a listener as you can be for 90 seconds. Go!"

Review discussion
6–12 minutes

"How many *B*'s had *A*'s who already showed super listening ability? What can we say about this practice time? Was anything hard? New?"

"Okay, that's enough for now. I just wanted to get us started on what I call tutor training. It's training so you can be better helpers for one another in our class. Next time I ask you to help one another, stretch yourself toward excellent listening skills."

Step 2: Review

After a day or so, review this listening lesson, perhaps simply by prompting a whole-class discussion with some questions: "Has anyone become more aware of good and poor listening since we had our practice? Has anyone practiced becoming a more skillful listener? How many of the three good listening skills can you now list on scrap paper? How many listed one? Two? Three? Please continue practicing here or out of school." Or try the Like/Might strategy:

"Think back to times when you listened to others in the last day or so in this class, in other classes, at home, anyplace. As you think about the listening you did, write one or two things you *liked* about it, such as, 'I liked the way I focused my attention on the person I was listening to.'

"Now as you think back to those listening experiences, see if you can write a sentence that begins 'Next time I might. . . .' You could write about doing things better, or differently, or anything else. Not a promise that next time you *will*, just a sentence about what you *might* do next time.

"Would anyone like to share some of their notes with the class?"

Step 3: Practice Pairs

A few days after the above exercise, conduct another set of practice pairs, this time focusing on disciplining urges to upstage others—that is, holding back one's own thoughts when others are speaking:

"*A*'s, please pick a topic that you have pretty strong feelings about. For instance, what parents, teachers, police, or the President should do or not do; what's wrong with this town or school. Tell *B* your topic.

"*B's*, you start this practice. Your job is to pretend your opinions are very different from *A's*. I'll give you two or three minutes to tell your 'different' opinions to *A*. Speak as if you really mean it, with dignity and power, the best you can.

"*A's*, your job is to practice good listening. And to practice not upstaging the person who is speaking. Not interrupting. Not taking away that person's right to speak up. Not showing disrespect to the person. Put your own ideas on the shelf and just listen. While *B* speaks, (1) aim to look pleasantly at *B*, (2) give *B* plenty of time to think about what to say, and (3) do not interrupt. If you feel the need to say anything, say something like 'Yes, I think I understand how you feel.' Or try a brief summary of an idea your partner expressed, for instance, 'As I hear it, you feel parents should never ground teenagers.' Ready? Go!"

Step 4: Review

A few days later, review as before, using an Attentive Discussion strategy or the Like/Might Review strategy:

"Has anyone become more aware of holding back your thoughts when others are speaking? Has anyone become more aware of people who interrupt others when they're speaking? Has anyone risked practicing this self-discipline skill? Please be aware of this skill and keep practicing it, because it will help us be good tutors."

Step 5: Brainstorming

I take a new tack in the fifth and last step in tutor training:

Introduction and pair/ trio brainstorming. *3–5 minutes*	"Some people are good at tutoring. What do they do? Well, they may ask the person they're tutoring how they can best help. Or they may ask, 'Am I going too fast?' or 'Do you want to take a break now or try some new practice problems?' Please sit with one or two of your classmates and brainstorm a list of some of the things that good tutors do. You can include my ideas or any others. Go."
Group reporting and class summary. *10–15 minutes*	"Let's see if we can agree on the four or five most important things that tutors do. Too many items will give us too much to keep in

mind as we try to be better tutors. Each
group start by giving one idea for our board
list. Then we'll vote and see which we agree
are most important. Finally, I'll ask one or
two of you to make us a wall chart, so we
can occasionally review our Guidelines for
Good Tutoring."

After Training

Soon after training, if a real tutoring situation did not arise, I might
invent a mini-practice exercise:

"Please pair up now with someone you do not usually sit
with. One of you be *A* and the other, *B*. I'd like you to pretend
that you are not sure how to do long division. *B*, your job is to
be a good tutor and help your partner learn how to do long
division. You might look at our Guidelines for Good Tutoring.
I'll give you just three or four minutes for this tutoring practice.
Then we'll look back and see what we can learn from it. Then
we'll reverse roles and try again."

It's important here to pick subject matter that both students are likely
to understand fairly well. It is less important that the content be relevant
to the class. I have asked tutors to help their partners learn how to add
fractions, how to memorize three spelling words, how to remember
what they read in a book, how to get from the school to the post office.

After the practice session, review by asking each person to write
some outcome sentences and then have students share them using the
Whip Around, Pass Option strategy. Finally, use the Learning Challenge
strategy (see page 78):

"I challenge you to keep stretching yourself toward tutoring
excellence and toward excellent communication outside class.
If you accept this challenge, keep track of your progress. If you
have a difficult communication situation to deal with, perhaps
ask a friend to be one of your cheerleaders. And from time to
time, let me and your classmates know what progress you are
making."

Strategy 9.7: Student Procedure Mastery

Description: Spending enough time teaching classroom procedures so students will be able to follow them easily and efficiently.

Purpose: To eliminate the need to repeatedly explain classroom procedures to students.

It is tempting to assume that students will understand and follow simple procedures such as "Pick a partner and talk over last night's homework" or "Put your folder on the shelf in alphabetical order." But some students will neither comprehend well nor follow directions smoothly. The remedy? Overteach procedures, especially when teaching elementary school students. Aim for all students to have absolute mastery of procedures and to feel good about that mastery. For young students, it's often wise to walk through a procedure, giving explicit instructions, as illustrated here:

> "When I say 'Get a partner,' first look around and make eye contact with someone. You can sit with someone nearby or not, as you choose. But if I ask you to pick someone you haven't worked with recently, you may have to get up and walk to another part of the room to make that eye contact. Then sit close enough to the person so that you can talk quietly.
>
> "Let's try that. Pick a partner you haven't worked with recently and sit together."
>
> After students begin to get settled, the teacher says, "Let's talk about this. Chances are, some of you felt anxious about being left out, anxious about asking someone to be your partner, to take the risk and ask. As I look around, I see that some of you were in fact left out. It was tempting to make a trio instead of a pair. Or to sit by yourself. Or to come and ask me what to do. Please go back to your original seats and let's try this again.
>
> "This time, when I say 'Go,' take a risk and do not rush to sit with the first person you see. If most are paired up and you are still without a partner, look to see if anyone else is left alone. Someone else may not have felt like taking a risk today, so you may find someone sitting quietly alone. That sometimes happens. Take your time and look closely, like a detective looking for someone. If you have done that and still find no one without a partner, please form a trio. Ask a pair if you might join them.
>
> "Let's try it again. Please get yourself a partner you haven't worked with recently. Go."

Similarly, the instruction "Talk over last night's homework," invites confusion, which invites noncompliance, which invites discipline problems. I've seen teachers use charts like this one to remind students of what they should be doing:

Homework Groups
- Compare answers.
- Talk through disagreements.
- Help each other understand.
- Check with another group if unsure.
- Support each other in mastering the content.

Here's a chart that one teacher uses when right-wrong answers are not central to the assignment and she wants to remind students of what they should be doing as they're giving feedback on writing assignments:

Guidelines for Giving Feedback on Writing Homework
1. Exchange papers.
2. Read thoughtfully.
3. Make helpful feedback notes.
4. If there is time, talk over your reactions.

The point is that teachers should spend enough time to make procedures perfectly clear and acceptable to all. Take the time to help students enjoy their ability to follow guidelines masterfully and smoothly. The initial investment of time is well worthwhile because it will likely save many hours over the entire school year.

10 Homework Strategies

The word "homework" brings as much joy to the average student as a toothache. For teachers, too, homework is often a tedious, tiresome chore. Yet homework can be one of our most efficient, flexible, and potent tools for learning—if we know how to use it.

Strategy 10.1: Assignment with Choice

Description: An assignment that includes student choice.

Purpose: To maximize student learning and help students develop self-responsibility.

Teachers often assign homework that offers students little choice in what to do: "Do the first ten problems on page 36." "Read Chapter 10 and be ready for a test on it." The advantage to such assignments is that we know exactly what each student was supposed to do, which makes it easy to review the work later with the class as a whole. The disadvantages are that some students do more homework than they need to master the topic, others do less homework than would be good for them, and all miss chances to practice responsible self-management.

The Assignment with Choice strategy is fairly simple: offer students some choice in what they will do for homework. For instance:

- **Assign flexible amounts of homework.** "Do as many problems as you think you need to really learn the material well." "Read the chapter and write as many outcome sentences as you can." Or, "Do at least the first three problems, more if that would be good for you." The advantage to this kind of homework assignment is that students are regularly asked to consider what would be good for them. Regularly making that kind of decision in class prepares them to make the same decision in other situations, for instance, when their impulses or their friends are pushing them to do things that really are *not* good for them.

• **Assign homework that allows students to learn different material.** "Choose some difficult spelling words and practice writing them correctly." Or, "Discuss any three of the problems on page 74." Such assignments allow students to do more or less learning, as the material and their personal situations vary.

• **Use a flexible time assignment.** Encourage students to intelligently choose the amount of time they spend on homework. "Study the material for at least 20 minutes, more if that would be good for you." Or, "Decide how long you want to work on the assignment. Set a timer and then stick to your commitment and do it."

• **Ask students to create their own homework assignments.** "Design a homework assignment on this topic that you think would be good for you." Or, "Choose a partner and prepare homework assignments for each other. Later, exchange work and help each other check what you did."

Here are some examples of assignments collected from teachers I've worked with:

• Read Chapter 6 and write outcome sentences showing what you learned from the chapter.

• For tomorrow, read any story from our class library.

• Aim to create one or more real-life word problems based on this math work.

• From the list of words and phrases on the sheet distributed, be ready to read aloud as many as you can.

• For homework, please think back over today's class activities and write a Like/Might Review: First, list some things you *liked* about what you did, then see if you can list some things you *might* handle differently next time.

• On the board is a set of information. Draw as many conclusions as you can from that information and be ready to share it tomorrow with a partner. Afterward, I'll ask you to write outcome sentences.

The Long-Term Benefits of Assignments with Choice

Choice invites the bright or interested student to do more work, something students rarely do when assignments are without choice. More important, making choice part of homework assignments gives students real practice in learning to make wise choices for themselves.

I recommend periodically talking to students about the idea of making choices and how it fits in with doing homework. Here are a few examples of such talks:

Example 1. "You will notice that in this class almost all homework assignments will include a choice. Sometimes the choice will be to do *more or less* of an assignment, such as how many words to learn. Sometimes the choice will be whether to do *this or that*, such as whether you should study new words or review your old words. In addition, you will always have the choice of how *well* to do your homework.

"Perhaps the biggest choice you must make is whether to do the homework assignment at all. I can insist that you do it. But you and only you can choose to comply, to actually do it. No one else can live your life for you. Is it ever smart to skip a homework assignment entirely? I'd say yes, because more urgent matters do occasionally come up. Can anyone think of some examples of times like this?"

Example 2. "I believe doing homework is important. It is important for learning the subjects we're studying and also for developing self-discipline. I want you to do your homework, do it well and do it every day. But I also want you to live intelligently, not to do everything everyone tells you to do just because they said so.

"When I talk about intelligent choices here, I am not referring to your moods or doing easy work. Sometimes you will not feel like doing your work. And sometimes it will be very hard to stick with it and complete it. Is it intelligent to skip work in those situations? Why or why not?"

Example 3. "Because homework is valuable for learning and reviewing learning, you will have an assignment every day, from the first day of school to the last, including weekends. The homework will help you learn to manage your time out of school, too. I hope you're able to do this. I encourage you to manage your out-of-school activities so you can do at least the minimum homework assignment every day. What can you do to manage your time this way? Let's brainstorm some ideas.

"Even if you set aside time for homework, you may sometimes feel lazy or be distracted by something. That happens. But you can learn to say no to distractions. I encourage you to learn how to do that. One of the main jobs you have at this point in your life is your schoolwork. Yet we all have impulses and temptations that can distract us from our jobs. What are some distractions that might cause you or your friends to put off doing homework? What are some ideas for making it easier to say no to such impulses and temptations and to stick to your work?"

Example 4. "How *well* you do your homework is a choice you have to make. Have you noticed that you do some things more carefully than other things? I'm like that too. Can you think of some advantages to learning how to do careful work, work that you're proud of? Do you know any hints for making it easier to work carefully?"

After raising such points, it would not be wise to forget about them. They are important enough to call for review and reconsideration. Here are some questions you might follow up with later, though not all on one day:

• How many are finding that you are doing more than the minimum homework some days? Do you ever *not* do the minimum? How do you decide what is best for you to do?

• What ideas have you come up with for managing your time so you don't have to struggle every day to make time for homework? How many of you need more ideas or, perhaps, a support buddy to help you learn how to better manage your time?

• How many of you have been aiming not only to do homework, but to do it very well—that is, seriously and carefully, so you can be proud of it? How many of you are perfectionists with your homework, are never fully satisfied, and probably would be better off relaxing a bit with homework? What can we learn about this issue of striving too hard versus not striving hard enough?

• What are the temptations that are getting in the way of homework these days for you? Do you have any tricks to share that help you say no to temptations that would not be good for you?

• How many of you have already had a day when you found it was intelligent not to do any homework at all, when something else was really more important to do, when something made putting time into your homework not your best choice? Is anyone willing to share an example?

• Homework sometimes calls for persistence, "stick-to-it-iveness." How many of you are good at sticking to tasks, even when the tasks are not easy or pleasant? How many are not so good at that? I wonder if we could list some things on the board that help people persist. Do you want to try some of these ideas? How about telling a partner about your plan and how things have worked out for you.

When homework assignments give students choices, the discussions resulting from the questions listed above become especially appropriate and fruitful and may contribute to the development of learning skills ultimately more valuable than any academic homework.

Strategy 10.2: Homework Sharing Groups

Description: Groups (usually pairs) of students who sit together to review or correct homework.

Purpose: To maximize academic learning and promote self-responsibility.

This is a strategy for handling completed homework. It shifts the process away from making sure the work was done to using completed work to deepen and expand learning. The strategy calls on students to share their work in some way.

If the homework involves definite right and wrong answers, Learning Pairs may be used to review homework. Pairs of students compare answers, teach each other when confusions or errors arise and, if both are stuck, ask other pairs for assistance. When both students understand the material, you may ask students to create new problems for each other. (See Strategy 12.1 on page 155 for more information on Learning Pairs.)

For subjects in which correct answers are unlikely to be revealed by the process of comparing work, you might provide correct answers on the chalkboard or read aloud answers before the Homework Sharing Groups begin.

Here are some uses of this strategy I've received from other teachers:

• **From a junior high history teacher:** "I ask students to come to class each day with one or more outcome sentences related to their reading homework. Often, but not every class period, I ask students to sit in groups of four and take turns whipping around the group, sharing at least one of their outcome sentences and, after each has had a turn, informally discussing what they learned. I find students read more seriously and learn more when they have a few minutes to tell others what they learned. They hear others' perceptions, which are often different from their own. They hear about ideas they never thought about. They also seem to learn more and learn, too, that others' points of view are different and worth listening to."

• **From a 2nd grade teacher:** "I ask students to be ready each day to read at least one new paragraph to another student, and to read it with feeling and meaning. In class, I tell students to find a partner they have not read with recently and to take turns reading their paragraphs to each other. Partners are to listen and, afterwards, comment on how well they heard and understood the reading.

"I recommend students read from a storybook but allow them to read from anything they want. In the slow class, some even pick a comic book. One always reads from the daily newspaper! I want them to get in the habit of reading aloud whatever is meaningful to them. Some need to practice this many times at home to do well in class, and I send letters home that tell parents how I want them to help. Mainly, I say, do not push the child. Do not remind the child of that homework. Allow the child to ask for help. Do not *offer* help. Help the child learn responsible initiative. Then help the child read the paragraph until he or she feels comfortable and ready for the next day's oral reading. Do not tell a child when he or she is ready. Let children learn to judge that."

• **From a high school English teacher:** "I use Homework Sharing Groups to give students more feedback on their writing than I have time for. Sometimes I have students form pairs and read aloud to each other what they've written. Sometimes I have all students put their homework on my desk and then give students ten minutes to choose papers from the pile and write a critique in the margins, doing as many papers as time allows (some papers get more than one critique). I usually include lessons on how to be an informed critic and distribute a form headlined 'How to Be a Useful Critic.' Many students learn more from the critiquing process than they ever do from the writing process."

• **From a college teacher:** "I often ask students to prepare mini-lessons based on the knowledge they gained from their reading. In class, then, I have students form random trios, I set a timer for five minutes, and I tell students that each person has five minutes to give a mini-lesson to two peers. The student's task is to teach the other two students something about the material. The two listeners are to respect the time of the speaker and not interrupt with their own ideas. When the timer rings, the next person is the presenter. After all three have spoken, an extra five minutes is set so each trio can discuss ideas informally."

Homework sharing groups often benefit from occasional discussions of process: "How did the groups go today? How can we do better next time?" You may ask students to write Like/Might Review notes: "Today I liked the way I . . . " and "Next time I might. . . . " Note that teacher evaluation of homework is not part of this strategy. Learning takes place quite naturally, without any need for teacher evaluation. The desire of students to understand and share work naturally leads to learning. The emphasis here is on the *process* of learning, not on *what* was learned. The content is controlled by selecting what students are asked to read and share. The students are then left to manage the process. This process focus seems to produce the most learning for students and, not at all incidentally, serves the development of good lifelong learning habits.

Strategy 10.3: Homework Hearing

Description: A teacher meeting briefly with each student to hear about completed homework.

Purpose: To advance responsible work habits and give each student a bit of personal attention.

This strategy, adapted from Pilon (1991), gives each student a moment or two to report directly to you the work he or she has done. Let's look at how a high school biology teacher introduced this strategy in his class:

"As you know, part of the time on Fridays you will be in one or another work group. During that group time, I will take turns visiting each of your groups. When I join yours, please discontinue your work temporarily. Each of you, then, please take a moment to read me something from your homework journal. You can read me any one or two of your recent learnings or tell me about a question you have. Others will just listen in as you and I do this. This will give me a chance, each week, to visit with each of you personally. It will help me keep up with how you are doing."

An elementary school teacher used a different system for meeting with each student:

"As you saw, each day you will have time in which you will be working individually in the classroom, as when I give you individual study tasks. One thing I will do during that time is ask you to come to this sharing table, in alphabetical order. When you get here, you will have a chance to read me the words you mastered for homework. Here's the way it will work. I will be sitting at one side of the table. Opposite will be five chairs for five students. When you see a chair is empty, please temporarily move from your individual work to that empty chair and wait for your turn to read your homework words. I will hear the words from the student in the end chair. When that student is finished, he or she simply goes back to individual task work. When that happens, the other four students slide over. That's how a chair gets to be empty.

"Keep aware of when your name is coming up. If you are next in the alphabet, come over and sit in the empty chair. Have your homework with you, for when you eventually slide into the end chair, your job will be to read aloud, with as much confidence as you can muster, the words you worked on for homework. Let's walk through this procedure to get the idea more clearly."

Note that with this strategy the teacher speaks to one student at a time while other students sit nearby. This allows other students to listen in and, perhaps, learn something from the student-teacher dialogue. It also helps some students feel less intimidated than they might if they had to meet alone with a teacher. This strategy is also efficient, for it virtually eliminates empty time between student reports. Teachers say they can hear reports from 30 students in only 30 minutes.

How might you respond to students in these meetings? I recommend:

• **Easy eye contact.** We want each student to be clear that he or she has inviolable self-worth, an essential value, one that need not be earned. Warm and accepting eye contact can affirm that self-worth. When a student is ready to report to you, then, the first move I recommend is a look that is easy and accepting, inviting of whatever eye contact the student is willing to make. You need say nothing. Just look warmly into the student's eyes.

• **Supportive responses.** When a student gives a report, I recommend encouragement that does not rely on praise or rewards. I personally prefer to use "I Appreciate" messages, "I'm With You" statements, Plain Corrects, and Plain Incorrects.

• **Cushioning.** It is occasionally useful to use the Cushioning strategy in meetings, especially when a student who is reporting (or sitting nearby listening) may need a confidence boost, and also generally to inoculate against learning anxieties and to keep deepening learning confidence. Here are some examples:

— "Before you begin, Jill, I wanted to know if you think it would it be all right if you made mistakes in your homework." . . . If she answers "yes": "Why would that be all right?"

— "Clarence, before you start, tell me if you think it would be okay if you or anyone else did not understand a thing about the homework assignment, not one thing. . . . Why?"

— "You have no homework for today, Terry? Well, do you remember what the sign says? We each have our ways and time clocks, so that sometimes happens. Can you handle having your homework ready tomorrow?"

— "First off, Fritz, I want to ask you something. What if someone did not have time to learn this material yet? Can you think of a sign that would explain why that sometimes happens?" . . . "Thank you, now please tell me about your work for today."

• **Self-Management Stimulators.** I like to use occasional comments designed to stimulate attention to personal work habits. I've highlighted key phrases in the examples below:

— "You did more than the minimum required. *Do you feel good about yourself for having done that much?*" This might be followed by: "Thanks, Sue. I was just wondering."

— "It seems to me you did your work very carefully. *Did you deliberately choose to work very carefully this time?*" This might be followed by: "I see, Ned. I was just curious."

– "You have nothing to report for homework. That sometimes happens. *I wonder how you feel about not having work today, if you feel okay about it?*" This might be followed by: "Thanks, Bill. I just wanted to know."

– "You have nothing to report for homework. *Please take a moment and ask yourself if you are willing to do what it takes to have tomorrow's homework completed.*" Whether the student answers yes or no, respond with the following: "Thanks for thinking about that. I'll see you tomorrow."

– "You do your homework very well every day. *Is it hard for you to say no to temptations that want to distract you from your work?*" The response to the student's answer is: "Thanks. I was curious about that."

– "You have not done very much. *I wonder if you could use some hints or more support for managing your time or for saying No to impulses to be lazy. Can I or one of your classmates help in some way?*" Perhaps follow this with, "Would you be willing to ask for that help? And will you tell me how it worked out if you do get help?"

Self-management stimulators call for an artistic touch. If possible, I suggest joining with other teachers for practice and feedback until you feel comfortable with them. Note, however, that you need not use self-management stimulators to benefit from the Homework Hearing strategy. Self-management stimulators are simply extra nourishment.

Finally, remember that the focus of Homework Hearing is not on grading student work but on demonstrating that you respect the value of the homework students do. I recommend simply making mental notes of which students need extra help or which learnings need extra review.

It may be clear that this strategy gives each student a minute or two of personal, fully respectful attention. I believe that regular doses of such attention can pull many children out of self-doubt and self-denigration and can help them develop the self-esteem essential to productive living.

Here's what a high school Spanish teacher had to say about his experience with this strategy:

> I changed my approach to homework. I decided I wanted all students to know they were not less worthy if and when they

did not do homework. Since, in Spanish, homework is *very* important, this was a *very* risky experiment for me. But I did it and guess what? Eventually students started doing more—not less—homework. They also did it more willingly. I no longer struggle with students about homework, although I still find myself slipping. I must learn patience with students even as I am beginning to appreciate how I can teach them to be more patient with themselves. Something about once a week giving each student a chance to show me what they learned without worrying that I will judge the work or correct or in any way be critical has changed something important for us all. Now they *like* to show me their stuff.

Strategy 10.4: Homework Unlike Classwork

Description: Homework assignments distinctly different from classroom activities.

Purpose: To make homework more interesting to students.

Many students find homework uninteresting simply because it too closely resembles the work they do in class. One remedy for this problem is to design homework assignments that are related to classwork but require students to use different skills than they used in class. Here are some possibilities:

• Ask students to make up new problems that might be used for class drills.

• Ask students to draw something that illustrates an idea related to the classwork.

• Ask students to pick one or more words mentioned in class and look them up in a dictionary or encyclopedia or ask someone in the neighborhood about them. Ask students to write down what they discover.

• Ask students in an English class to cut out parts of speech from magazines or newspapers.

• Ask students to write each day at least one new sentence in their journals.

11   Testing and Grading Strategies

The traditional methods of testing and grading please few who are touched by them. Teachers say they take too much time and energy. Many students and parents complain they are inaccurate and unfair. Yet they continue to be used and, in most schools, are unlikely to soon change in any fundamental way. I recommend, therefore, that teachers proceed slowly in moving beyond common testing and grading practices. Unless you are prepared to handle much criticism, focus on improving teaching and simply do your best to minimize the problems of the testing and grading system. The strategies in this chapter are designed to help you do that. In general, they serve three purposes:

• They take the emphasis off grade getting (the central concern of so many students) and put more emphasis on learning and developing good lifelong learning habits.

• They reduce discouragement among those students slow to earn the top grades, the ones so often tempted to give up even *trying* to do well.

• They reduce the time needed for testing and grading by providing more ways to assess student progress while students are learning, so we need not spend so much time on testing that does little to promote learning.

Note that in Chapter 2, I discussed one valuable testing strategy, **the Review Test,** that serves those purposes. It involves posing a review question, asking all students write to down an answer at their desks, then announcing the correct answer or writing it on the board. Students check their work and, if necessary, make corrections. There is no grading involved. Please refer to the complete explanation of this strategy in on page 46.

Strategy 11.1: Portfolio

Description: A collection of student work.

Purpose: To increase self-responsible student learning and to provide evidence for evaluation by the teacher.

Portfolios are simply collections of student work that students manage for themselves. In an elementary class, for instance, each student might have a folder containing collected writings, worksheets, and drawings. At the end of each week, students might be asked to sort through the folder, write some outcome sentences based on the week's papers, star the items they feel best about, and perhaps select any they want to bring home to show families.

Portfolios develop self-management abilities, reduce the need to test students, and are broadly adaptable on many grade levels. They can be used as a supplement to testing or as the core of an evaluation plan. Dennie Palmer Wolf has many excellent suggestions for the use of portfolios you may want to explore. I've included several of her writings in the Recommended Resources for Chapter 11 on page 189.

Here are recommendations for portfolio development that I distribute to college students beginning a teacher training program:

Self-Managed Evaluation Process

Many college students are accustomed to asking about requirements and then going about fulfilling them. That approach does not empower learners or learning; it serves passivity and uncritical obedience. This is *not* the approach our faculty intends. Our commitment is to instruct in ways that strengthen people, that expand their ability to learn intelligently and responsibly. We are also committed to reducing disconnections, disconnections between courses and between what is learned and what happens in real life.

A key element in our approach is the student portfolio. This is a request for you to take responsibility for building one for yourself. We recommend you build it with three purposes in mind:

1. To organize and integrate the whole of your work, so you can clearly track your progress and interests.

2. To reflect on your current experiences and the choices ahead, so you can maximize the amount and the relevance of your learnings.

3. To keep your work in a coherent and tangible form, so your progress can be communicated to the faculty.

Portfolios are meant to be self-designed and self-managed. As you begin building yours, consider including some of the elements described here:

Personal goals. This section consists of notes about your long- and short-term targets. You might begin simply by listing a few broad goals and some goals that focus on teaching. For the teaching goals, you might include:

• Knowledge goals: what you want to understand. For example, why some people don't learn, what B. F. Skinner proposed, how values are developed.

• Skill goals: what you want to be able to do. For example, get a job, handle misbehavior, avoid overwork, get appreciated, keep all students involved all the time.

• Being goals: how you want to *be* as you do what you do. For example, be flexible, be confident, be empathetic, be caring, be optimistic, be assertive.

Experience log. This section consists of a list of significant experiences related to your professional growth. Perhaps list courses you took, books and other materials you read, conversations that were meaningful, experiments you tried, family events that made a difference.

Learning log. This section is devoted to tracking your professional development, usually by indicating goals that you have met and new goals that are emerging. You might also include a section that identifies what you were able to extract from your experiences, perhaps by keeping diary-like entries of sentences with such beginnings as:

• I learned . . .
• I am beginning to wonder . . .
• I was surprised . . .
• I rediscovered . . .
• I now better appreciate . . .
• I now promise to . . .
• I have become skillful at . . .
• I uncovered a new question about . . .
• I reevaluated my assumptions about . . .
• I was proud of the way I . . .

You may find it useful to set up categories for these learnings, such as *psychological principles, useful references, teaching methods, ideas for units of study,* and so on.

Supporting items. Your portfolio might also include a table of contents and examples of work you produced. Perhaps include papers you've written, summaries of different theories that interested you, tapes of yourself teaching at different points in your program, or feedback forms from students.

In many cases, you will want to have a home reservoir of materials from which you can assemble an easily transportable version of your portfolio to share with others when appropriate. In all sections of the portfolio, unless the faculty directs otherwise, say as little or as much about any element as serves your best interests.

Note this special request: Please treat your portfolio as a learning tool. Do not highlight its use as an assessment tool. Do not build a portfolio to impress the faculty, for that may erase much of its power to serve you. It may even erase some of your own respect for learning and growing. You will occasionally be invited to show parts of your portfolio to the faculty, so they can assess your work more accurately. And you may occasionally be asked to create and include special items, such as a summary of your learnings to date or a list of current interests and needs. But you will never be asked to reveal parts of your portfolio that you choose to keep private. If you want to impress the faculty, use your portfolio to demonstrate your sincere, steady, intelligent striving to get the most from your learning experiences.

Strategy 11.2: Grading Plan

Description: A plan for grading that considers both the teacher's current grading responsibilities and the students' long-term welfare.

Purpose: To spend more time on learning and less on grading.

Most teachers give grades, but what is the best way to do so, especially if you care not only about what students learn now but also about how they will conduct their adult lives? I recommend that you keep in mind the limits of what is feasible, which will vary from school to school and according to your own readiness to take risks, and then consider adaptations of common practices. Here are some adaptations that many teachers have found valuable and workable:

Minimum testing. After students have been in class for a few weeks, and assuming you do more than lecture, you can usually tell quite accurately who is learning much and who is learning little. You may need to look at students' outcome sentences, homework papers, portfolio items, or other such material, but you rarely need many *tests* to identify high achievers and low achievers.

If you give occasional tests, less to scare students into studying than to give them chances to summarize and show their stuff, you will almost certainly have enough data to scale learners into grading categories. This is the minimum-test approach I generally recommend. It does not rely on tests alone, but on all the data available, objective and subjective. You and your students are then free to spend more time on learning and less on testing.

Professional responsibility statement. What if a student or parent comes to you and complains, "You cannot rely on subjective judgment. I want to see hard evidence that supports your grades." How do you respond? I favor telling the truth: "I want to spend more time on learning and less on grading. I use all experiences in the classroom to determine how much each student is learning. Over time I can judge how well most students are doing and, when I am unsure, I simply look for more data."

If this explanation does not satisfy the person, I might add a statement stirred by my professional dignity: "I understand your concern that Gene be graded fairly. Yet, as a dedicated professional, I need to be trusted with my judgments. It would diminish my ability to teach if I had to take the time to collect and document the data everyone would like to see. I hope you will trust that I am competent to make these kinds of judgments. You're welcome to visit my class. I'm sure you'll see that learning is taking place and that I am aware of what students are doing. And please speak to the school administrators if you would like to be sure they trust me to judge my students fairly."

Being criticized is uncomfortable, as is worrying about defending your grading judgments. It is tempting to avoid confrontations about grading, even when it means using more time and energy for evaluation than you believe is necessary. Professionally and personally, I prefer doing the best job I can in the classroom and being prepared to call up my courage when necessary to respond to criticism. When I have implemented new grading practices, I've sat down and consciously thought about how I would defend them to parents and others. I've even written down complete statements to bolster my resolve. You may want to do the same.

The up-grade option. You can relax many students' preoccupation with grading—and get them attending that much more to learning— simply by making each individual grade earned less significant. Some teachers accomplish this by collecting large numbers of grades, perhaps for daily work, weekly tests, and monthly reviews, so no single grade is critical. However, rather than divert attention from grading, this approach actually seems to focus more attention on it. It certainly adds to teachers' noninstructional chores.

An alternative is to collect fewer grades and make any one of them less significant by allowing students to do extra work when they do not like the grade earned. "If you would like to improve your grade," a teacher might say to students, "write a contract saying what you would like to do to earn extra credit. If I okay your proposal, and you do what I judge to be quality work on your up-grade project, you will get the grade you want."

The certain make-up. I favor telling students that they can always make up missed work. I sometimes insist, however, that students find their own helpers or tutors, which they usually can do from within the class. Compared with penalizing students for work avoided or missed, this approach seems to me less punitive, more respectful, and more in tune with my concern for the development of self-management. Some say this is coddling, but I do not think so. Making up work missed, like doing extra work to raise a grade, is not easy in our busy world, especially when new work demands keep pressing on students' time.

Goal agreement. Many students are accustomed to hearing a teacher announce course expectations, content to be covered, require- ments, and the like. It is possible to offer these, invite course agreement, and then ask students if they want to create some of their *own* expecta- tions for the course:

> " . . . That is what I would like you all to do. Are you willing to go along with that? How about starting this way and later looking again to see how we all feel about this course outline?

"Also, I wonder if you can find any goals of your own related to the focus of this class. If you have personal goals, there is a chance we can find ways to help you reach them. You might, for example, write a personal learning contract. Or we might set up groups to help you reach your goals. Do you want to search for some personal goals right now?"

When students agree on the goals of a course, grading that is tied to meeting those goals will likely proceed amicably. If the goals you proposed have become the personal goals of your students, students will more likely see you as someone on their side rather than someone there simply to judge them. You might even arrive at grades cooperatively with students. Most significantly, perhaps, you will be advancing the idea that learners must take responsibility for their own learning.

Procedure agreement. Sometimes you can seek agreement with students on procedures that affect grading:

• "Here are several samples of what I consider excellent work. Let's study these together so my definition of excellence is clear."

• "As for rating your work, here is what I propose . . . Any suggestions for improving that process? Are you willing to go along with it, at least for now, until we find something better we can agree on?"

Incidentally, I do not recommend giving credit for participation in class discussions. Some students naturally speak out in class and others learn better when they can relax and just observe. It seems to me unfair, an indignity really, to tell quiet people they must speak up or suffer a grading penalty. After all, we each have our own ways of learning.

Strategy 11.3: Focus-on-Learning Statement

Procedure: Explaining that the focus in the class is on learning, not on grading, and inviting students to adjust accordingly.

Purpose: To build a new emphasis on learning openly and respectfully.

Some teachers find it valuable to state openly to students that they intend to focus the class more on learning and less on grading, and to discuss this carefully enough so students are prepared to be active partners in achieving it.

A simple way to begin this strategy is to pose a question like this: "How can we take some of the heat out of testing and grading and give more of our attention to serious learning?" Usually, however, a more detailed approach works better, as in the classroom experience depicted here. It was related to me by a junior high mathematics teacher experienced in the approach advocated in this book:

> "Many students are preoccupied with grades," I said to my students. "For some it's more important to get a good grade than to learn something. How many of you feel a bit like that? Who would be willing to risk sharing their thoughts?"
>
> Several students responded to my question, and I listened to each of them, responding with comments like "Yes, I can understand that."
>
> "I'd like us to take a different approach in this class. I'd like us to focus on studying and learning, and to keep testing and grading in the background. This might be a difficult switch for some of you. After all, it's pleasant to get a good grade, and when we please our families with a good grade, everyone is happy. But there is a downside to a testing-grading focus. Take a few minutes now and each of you think of one or more downsides of testing and grading. Make notes for yourself and then let's see if we can make a group list on the chalkboard."
>
> The students worked for a few minutes and then we listed most of what they had come up with on the chalkboard:
>
> - Lots of us don't get good grades.
> - Grading makes us anxious.
> - We waste time studying for a test when we forget right away.
> - It's uncomfortable getting better grades than your friends.
> - Makes some of us sick.
> - Some are not good at taking tests.
> - Wastes a lot of class time.
> - It makes us feel bad when we fail.
> - Keeps our parents on our backs.
> - It makes some of us not want to come to class.
> - Makes some want to cheat.
>
> "I do have to give grades in this class," I said, "but I'd like to take the emphasis off the grades. Actually, I do not need many tests to know how much each of you is learning. After a while, as I keep working with you, I can tell. That's how I know what I need to reteach and when we can move on to a new topic: I watch and listen. You, too, probably can tell how much you are learning. You don't need lots of tests to tell you.

"I may want to have a test from time to time, not because I need to be sure how much you learned, but because a test can be a good way to pull a unit together. Tests like that won't hurt us—as long as we know that tests are not the main thing. An occasional test may even help some of you keep your attention on your classwork. There are lots of out-of-school pressures and temptations, after all, and pressures from other classes, too. If we had *no* pressure here, some of you might not be able to resist putting all your energy into something other than the work I need you to do here. Do any of you fall into that category?"

Several students raised their hands.

"Is it okay with you to have some tests, but not a lot?"

The students smiled and nodded their heads in agreement.

"Now, let's talk about grading. I do not want some students to feel they are better than others. I like you all. I respect you all. I know you all have lots of goodness inside you, probably more than even you yourself know right now. I do not want grades to come across as labels of more goodness and less goodness.

"There is the matter of time clocks too. Our posted signs remind us that we all learn some things now and some things later anyhow, so why get too anxious about it? You may zip ahead in your math learning later this year or even next year. That sometimes happens. It is more likely to happen if you do not get discouraged when your time clock for learning says you aren't ready now and just keep working hard at learning anyhow, doing the best you can now do.

"Yet, as I said, I must give grades. So here is what I propose. Think about what I'm saying, and if it does not feel right to you, let me know privately sometime soon. Then we'll talk and see if we can come up with a different plan the two of us can live with. Here is how I propose to start: First of all, I will give all who show up in class regularly and who keep doing the best they can a passing grade, at least a C.

"My job is to help you get into learning. If I cannot do my job well, or if your time clock for learning is different, or if other things are more important in your life at the time, well, that's no one's fault. That's just the way things were at the time. We all might be able to do better in the future. There's no sense in giving someone a grade lower than a C and making anyone feel bad because of it. That will do more harm than good, I think, especially since the grade you get in this course will not qualify you or disqualify you for anything very important. Of course, I couldn't say that if this was a course in piloting airplanes!

"I will give an extra good grade, which I call a B, for work that I feel is extra good. Does that mean that B grades are better than C grades? Not necessarily. It may just mean that those getting B grades had time clocks that allowed them to get extra good learnings. Or maybe our class methods just suited them.

"I will give a top grade, an A, to work that is a clear step ahead of extra good work, for work that seems to me outstanding. Are people who get A's better people than people who get B's and C's? Who can guess why I would say no?"

Nearly all the students pointed to the sign *We each learn in our own ways, by our own time clocks.*

"Some people may not really *want* to deemphasize tests and grades. They still want to view grades as very important. I can accept that. I just want to reduce the time and energy that testing and grading take away from learning in our class.

"One other point: Looking at tests and grades in this new way will, I think, help you learn without worrying that you will not succeed. And when you worry less, chances are you will learn more and enjoy math more.

"Here's the plan: Get into your classwork. Give it your all. Forget about grading. And then let's see after a while what grade I think best fits your learning. If you are not satisfied with that grade, I'll mark down an 'I,' for 'in progress' or leave the grade blank and explain that your work is still in progress.

"Then you and I can plan what extra work you need to do to earn a grade that's more satisfying to you. But be careful: This will mean extra work while you have your regular work to do. But if you're willing to expend that extra effort, I'm willing to offer you the opportunity to get a different grade.

"Let's try this system for a while. If problems come up, speak to me privately or, if you think it better, let's talk about it with the whole class. I'll bet we can brainstorm a creative remedy to any problem that comes up. For now, though, let's put aside any problems you think you will have and give this way of working a try. I will point out errors in your work, but I won't grade papers. I won't grade homework. I won't grade class participation. I'll just react in ways that I think might help you learn better, because learning is what this class is all about."

Unlike the teacher in this example, some teachers are not willing to give a passing grade to students who come to class every day and work diligently at learning but master little material. I recommend that such teachers simply tell students their own requirements for a C grade. You can deemphasize grading and testing while also insisting on minimum competence for a passing grade.

I recommend that teachers who wish to conduct a discussion like the one above share their proposed approach beforehand with other teachers and, if appropriate, with administrators, asking for feedback and suggestions. It is not easy to move far from the current assumptions people carry about the importance of tests and grades. As with any change from old habits, the more support you have, the better.

Do not underestimate the time that students, parents, and you yourself will need to become comfortable with a focus shift away from grading and toward learning. Good grades have become an addiction for many people. You may need occasionally to restate your concerns and support those who are having difficulty breaking old habits. Fortunately, the truth is on your side, for the core purpose of schooling is indeed learning, not grading. You are not apt to proceed for long without finding others who will support your efforts. But you must not be so naive as to expect your plans to please everyone. They will not. I recommend you be clear about your intentions and strong in your professional commitment. You will likely need to call up courage.

Once you've discussed your approach to grading and testing with your class, as in the example above, give the issue minimum class time. The more attention given to grades and tests, the more prominent and convoluted the problems associated with them will likely become. The less talk about grading in the classroom, the better.

This issue of testing and grading is related to the issue of retaining failing students at grade level. In the long run, retention rarely helps students learn more. What it very often does do is diminish self-esteem. In all but the few cases in which everyone agrees retention best serves the particular student, I favor promotion for all students.

Strategy 11.4: Report Card Plan

Description: Planning to handle report cards in a way responsive both to professional requirements and the best interests of students.

Purpose: To make the report card a truly useful indicator of student progress.

Report cards are the central symbol of an evaluation system. A "good" report card reflects a successful academic experience, not necessarily a successful learning experience. And a "bad" report card often reflects trouble originating in the home rather than in the classroom. Here are some suggestions for making report cards less problematical and more reflective of a dignified learning community:

Progress conferences. Individual student-teacher conferences can effectively supplement the report card and diminish its importance and its potential for negative side effects. Some teachers set aside a few days regularly for such dialogues, which usually take place while other students are working on classroom tasks. A teacher might ask each student to bring to the conference notes about recent progress. The teacher's comments in the conference might proceed along these lines: "How has learning proceeded for you?" . . . "Here's how I see it." . . . "Any ideas about what you or I might do in the future?" . . . "All things considered, what grade should we list for this work?"

An open-door visitor policy. Inviting parents and other community members to visit and see the class in normal operation is another valuable way to show how students are progressing. When visitors see that students are working hard, most conclude that learning is taking place and there's no need to ask teachers to do more. Parents, then, become less concerned about report cards, and community members become more supportive of the school.

The open-door policy is simple: Any adults can observe at any time for as long as they like. Only if this practice becomes burdensome would I suggest that visitors make appointments. I suggest preparing a standard sheet of "Hints for Visitors" that a student committee, or the student of the day, could give to each visitor. The sheet might also include options for doing more than observing. A teacher might, for example, invite observers to tutor students who seem stuck or to participate directly in the students' learning activities.

Open Report cards. Sometimes the report card currently used by a school puts us in a difficult professional position. It may prompt us to communicate more discouraging or failing messages, for example, than would be good for students. In terms of DESCA, it is difficult, then, to avoid dignity damage, to avoid sending a negative message: *You are a failure as a person.* Or to avoid discouraging growth or self-management, suggesting: *It matters not what you say about your work.* Or to avoid fostering envy rather than class community: *Some students did far better than you.* Or to avoid narrowing student awareness: *Only what is listed here is worth your attention.*

It is sometimes wise to campaign for an improved report card. What kind of report card best avoids sending such messages? In general, cards more open and less restrictive, cards allowing flexible or subjective comments. Current learning and long-term living is almost always better served when teachers have more rather than fewer options for writing about a particular student's work. This is an instance in which restrictive requirements and precision are usually counterproductive.

Reverse report cards. Pilon (1991, p. 198) has suggested initiating what might be called "reverse report cards." These are cards from parents to teachers. Teachers could start by defining student behaviors they would like to promote. For instance, in an elementary class, these behaviors might include:

- Engages in self-initiated reading.
- Makes use of new vocabulary words when speaking.
- Handles everyday calculations willingly and accurately.
- Listens respectfully to what others say.
- Expresses self in some artistic ways.
- Walks and speaks with dignity.
- Maintains comfortable energy flow through the whole day.
- Manages own time and materials appropriately.
- Shows willingness to share and participate with others.
- Lives with awareness of things and people.

Teachers then could send parents a card listing those student behaviors and ask parents to watch for changes in them. Each marking period, the parents would return the card, noting which behaviors they've observed and perhaps writing down any other noteworthy changes they've observed in their children. Teachers would then have valuable data for class planning. They would know what students are learning in ways that show up in real life, at least as the parents report it. And perhaps they would know also what more is needed for certain students or for the whole class. The reverse report card may also help parents feel they are full partners in the learning process.

A similar system could be set up to ask each student to report on progress. Again, the data collected would be valuable for teacher planning. Such a system would invite students to take more responsibility for their progress and could serve well in private teacher-student progress conferences.

12 Strategies for Reviewing and Mastering Information

Most students need plenty of review to master subject matter. The strategies in this chapter are designed to help teachers provide review without being repetitious or boring. In Chapter 2, "Basic Instructional Strategies," I presented two valuable review strategies. I won't describe them here again, but you may want to review:

- The **Review Test strategy,** on p. 46.
- The **Choral Work strategy,** on p. 34.

Strategy 12.1: Learning Pairs

Description: Students working in pairs to help each other learn.

Purpose: To review and strengthen learnings and build interdependence among students.

In the Underexplain with Learning Pairs strategy introduced in Chapter 2, pairs of students collaborate to learn material the teacher has deliberately underexplained. Learning Pairs can also be used for review purposes. Students might, for example, drill each other on material to be memorized, perhaps using flash cards containing math facts or words from spelling lists. Or students might explain their understanding of material to each other and help each other with parts they don't understand. Students may base such work on an outline of information or on questions from a text.

In some cases, you may want to assign students to Learning Pairs to ensure slower students get the best help. In addition, you may want to instruct pairs to ask other pairs for assistance. If Class Tutors have been identified, they may also be called upon for assistance.

I find it useful to distinguish this function of pairs from the Sharing Pairs strategy. The task of Sharing Pairs is simply to compare and share ideas, as when students share completed homework or brainstorm ideas for a problem. Learning often results from Sharing Pairs activities, but students are not charged with the responsibility for learning. In Learning Pairs, however, learning is students' core responsibility, and I encourage students to do their best to help each other achieve it.

Strategy 12.2: "I Say" Review

Description: Pairs of students sharing what they have to say about a certain subject.

Purpose: To review and strengthen learnings and increase student cooperation.

Some students feel pressured and become anxious when I ask them to pair up and help each other learn, say, a list of vocabulary words. They may worry that they will not learn the material fast enough or as good as their partner learns it. An anxiety then grows that typically cuts into learning ability. To lessen student anxiety, I often use a form of Sharing Pairs, as in this example:

> "Pair up and take turns telling your partner what you have to say about each of the vocabulary words. For instance, let's say a boy and girl sit together and the first word is *light*. The boy might start and say what he thinks light is. Then the girl would say what she thinks light is. You could even talk about differences if you like. Then the boy says something about the next word. And so on. Or, if you prefer, one of you could say something about the first five words and then the other could say something about those five words. Go back and forth in a way that is good for both of you. Share what each of you has to say about each word. I'll give you a one-minute warning when it's time to stop. Go."

Asking pairs to share what each has to *say* about a word, rather than asking them to talk about the *correct* definition, usually produces a relaxed, thoughtful exchange. Students quite naturally talk about what the correct definition is, but the anxiety often associated with trying to get the right answer is absent.

I find that the "I Say" Review strategy often produces more learning more pleasurably than does the Learning Pairs strategy, with its emphasis on mastery. And it can be used with almost any content: a list of formulas, a list of people, a list of important events, a list of places, a list of science principles.

Strategy 12.3: Pass the Q&A

Description: The teacher announcing a question and an answer and all students passing the question and answer along, with one student asking the question, the next answering it.

Purpose: To emphasize a particular learning.

Pass the Q&A can be a fun way to reinforce a worthwhile learning. Used early in a class session, it also focuses and enlivens student energy. I once saw teacher Janet McCann addressing her 1st grade class. She said, "The question today is: *Is this black history month?* And the answer is: *Yes, this is black history month.*"

She then stooped so she was face-to-face with the boy in the first seat in the first row. She looked him in the eye and asked, "Is this black history month?"

The boy replied, "Yes, this is black history month," and promptly turned to the girl behind him and asked, "Is this black history month?"

The girl replied, "Yes, this is black history month," and she then turned to the student behind her and asked, "Is this black history month?"

And so it went. Each student in turn asked the question and heard the answer, down the row, passing along the Q&A.

Meanwhile, Ms. McCann started the same process with the first student in the second row, and then the remaining rows. As a result, within two or three minutes, every student had said aloud the question and the answer and had heard both several times.

When the last student had answered, Ms. McCann said, "Everyone now: Is this black history month?" And the class responded, "Yes, this is black history month."

What does this strategy do?

- It helps students absorb knowledge effortlessly.
- It raises the energy level of the class.
- It brings even restless students into a learning activity.
- It gives students a chance to practice looking others in the eye and speaking with personal power.

This strategy is from the work of Grace Pilon (1987a). I've seen it used to review a concept before going on to something new, and to insert a bit of worthwhile content that is not part of the curriculum, as in the black history example above, and simply as a way to zip up the energy level of students who have been silent a bit too long.

Teachers Comment

I use that strategy almost every day to get students to hear what proper language usage is. Many of them are being brought up in families in which proper usage is uncommon. The kids love it somehow. I use such Q&A's as "Did he and I go? Yes, he and I went." And "May I have permission? Yes you may." I also use the strategy to help them memorize authors, such as, "Who wrote Moby Dick? Herman Melville wrote Moby Dick." I think they like the idea of never being wrong. They hear the question and answer from me, and all they need to do is remember it for two minutes. Actually, I find most of them remember it long after! Repetition is the mother of remembering, or something like that.

—Junior High English Teacher

I sometimes use the Q&A pass strategy without an answer. I'll say in Spanish, "Turn to page 122," and have each student turn and pass the phrase down the line. I do sometimes use it with answers, to help them practice their speaking and to memorize vocabulary. For example, in Spanish I say, "If today is Monday, what is the next day? The next day is Tuesday." Then they pass that question and answer down the line.

—9th Grade Spanish Teacher

Strategy 12.4: Creative Reports ——————————————

Description: Student reports that are designed to be creative, not routine.

Purpose: To get student reports that actively involve listeners.

Reports of student work can sometimes serve as a useful review. Few activities, however, are less inspiring to a class than oral student reports. Small-group reports and, especially, individual book reports can quickly dull class awareness. Generally, I recommend avoiding all oral reports and, indeed, any activity that keeps students sitting passively for extended periods. Some report styles, however, can be inspiring indeed. Here are some possibilities you may want to use in your class:

One-minute reports. "Plan to tell us in 60 seconds about something you personally learned. We'll start each day with reports from five students. And we'll continue until we've all had a turn. And I'll give my own one-minute report each day."

Poster or model. "Create a poster, designed in any way you choose, that somehow reflects the book you read. Or make a model you can bring to class. We'll walk around and examine each person's poster or model Friday morning."

The group skit. "Present a skit related to something we learned about. Make it interesting, perhaps funny or dramatic. All members of your group must be involved in the presentation, so design it so you all have a part to play." When teachers use this to help students practice their writing skills, they will often ask them to write out their script, so the class can work on correct usage.

Book or history report. "Every day next week, we'll start with several of you acting out one of the persons we read about. Pick any person. Your job will be to wear something—a hat, a badge, anything that shows something about the person. The rest of us will then guess who you are. Or you can say something that person might have said and then we will guess. You can even team up with someone, get them to play a part, and act out a little skit showing something that person did or might have done."

Another group skit. "Have your skit show two different ways the character might have handled the situation." Or "Have your skit communicate something about either the growth or death of plants."

Pantomime or puppetry. "I'd like the report to include either pantomime or puppets." Or "Without words, act out a principle of science or the key learning you got from our unit."

Compact disc design. "Think of some song titles that might have come from those days and design a cover representing those songs, even though compact discs had not been invented then."

Dramatic reading. "Read something the person wrote and, as you read it to us, think the words, be fully into that person's character."

Mural. "I'd like each trio to produce one mural that shows different applications of what we studied."

Class activity. "Each pair is to get the class to do something that might be fun and that relates to the topic. Ask us, for example, to draw a pineapple with our eyes closed. Or to stand up and wave like an old tree about to topple over in the wind. Or create a fun five-minute quiz for us. The idea is to get us involved in your presentation."

Design. "Using only geometric figures, create a design that communicates something about the Civil War."

Collage. "This book report must be in the form of a collage. You can cut words or pictures or designs from old magazines or newspapers. You can even paste on small objects. In some creative way, aim to communicate an image or learning that you got from your book."

Short story. "Write a short story, funny or dramatic, that tells what you did and learned or that tells about people you studied. Put it in the story box with both your names on it. Include one blank sheet at the end of your story. Next month, when you have free time, pick a story from the box to read. If you have any reactions, note them on the blank sheet and include your name."

The Task Group, Share Group strategy described on page 102 also keeps all students actively involved in hearing about each other's work.

13

Strategies for Stimulating Thinking

Thinking is the royal road to meaningful learning. It is through thinking that we put random facts into useful contexts. And it is through thinking that we manage our own awareness and live intelligently. The strategies in this chapter are designed to aid you in helping students develop their thinking skills. You may also want to review the Outcome Sentences strategy on page 25, one of the most effective strategies for stimulating student thinking.

Strategy 13.1: Sort the Items

Description: Students placing items into categories specified by the teacher.

Purpose: To exercise critical thinking skills.

Here are some possible sorting tasks:

• Divide the list of foods into two groups, those with high calories and those with low calories.
  • Make pairs of synonyms from the list below.
  • Star the prime numbers on page 34.
  • Make a list of the carnivores illustrated here.
  • Identify the metaphors in the story.
  • Select the papers you wrote of which you are proud.
  • Pile the blocks that are not yellow or red.

To heighten student interest, Pilon (1984a, 1979, 1982, 1980, 1981, 1984b, 1986, 1988) recommends using materials students can physically manipulate. Consider this example of a girl completing a task involving such materials.

> Instructions the girl was given: "Select an envelope and lay out the cards it contains in any way that makes sense to you. Put together the cards you believe go well together."
>
> The girl spreads the cards from the envelope on the desk. She notices that most cards are white and contain common phrases: "in the house," "John went out," "hardly noticed." Two cards, however, are blue. One says "prepositional phrase." Another, "not prepositional phrase." She puts those two cards at the top of her desk. One by one, she puts the other cards under one of those headings. When she is finished, she asks a boy nearby to check her work. The boy, following instructions for this task, points at random to one of the cards and asks, "Did you have a reason for putting this one here?" The girl says, "'Under the tree' is a prepositional phrase." The boy says, "Thank you" and makes a check on the girl's record sheet to indicate she completed the task. The boy returns to his desk and the girl then puts the pieces back in the envelope and files the envelope and her record sheet.

Pilon has created several sets of cards like these, which she calls THINK-ERS®. They are highly engaging to students and effective for stimulating thinking for different academic subjects and different grade levels. There are enough of them so each student can to do one THINKER® each day of the year. THINKERS® are available from The Workshop Way Inc., P.O. Box 850170, New Orleans, LA 70185-0170.

Strategy 13.2: Classifying and Sorting ——————

Description: Students sorting items into categories they create themselves.

Purpose: To exercise critical thinking skills.

Because this strategy asks students to create their own categories for sorting rather than to simply place items into predetermined categories, it offers students a higher level thinking challenge than does strategy 13.1. It can be used in any subject area. A teacher might, for example, ask students to make groupings out of a list of spelling words, occupations, numbers written on the board, the words on page 202 of the index, the states in the United States, the items on a desk, or the battles of the Civil War.

Strategy 13.3 What's the Difference?

Description: Asking students how two or more items differ.

Purpose: To exercise skills of discrimination and perception.

This strategy involves simply asking students to identify the differences between two or more items. For instance, a teacher could ask students to compare verbs and adverbs, evaporation and absorption, hills and valleys, poems and songs. If you're at a loss for new items, pick two items from the index of a textbook. Here are some other suggested pairings:

English
- a colon and a semicolon
- a story and a joke
- Shakespeare and Hamlet
- a preposition and a proper name
- a formal letter and an informal note
- an incomplete sentence and a jail sentence

Social Studies
- a community and a country
- a leader and an elected official
- legislation and a legislator
- truce and peace
- ecology and environment
- a free election and a secret ballot

Miscellaneous
- surprise and delight
- a clock and a calendar
- a home and a house
- temperature and heat
- a fraction and a decimal
- a request and a question

- opinion and judgment and conclusion
- a wish and a hope
- an elephant and a box of cookies
- a square and a rectangle
- evaporation and perspiration
- inspiration and concentration

More thinking occurs when items are very similar, as in these examples:

- sad and sorrowful
- yard and meter
- boil and broil
- capitalism and free enterprise
- smart and intelligent
- wet and soaked

Strategy 13.4: What's the Same?

Description: Asking students how two or more items are the same.

Purpose: To exercise skills of discrimination and perception.

This strategy involves simply asking students to compare two or more items and describe how they are the same. For instance, you could ask students to compare clouds and mist, leaders and followers, eating good food and hiking tall hills. Any of the examples in Strategy 13.3 will also do.

You can make the challenge more difficult by choosing items that are very unlike each other and asking students to find similarities. For instance:

- one song and two zebras
- a liter and a letter
- Thursday and evaporation
- George Washington and long division
- compound interest and electricity
- newspapers and kindness

Strategy 13.5: Write a Summary

Description: Asking students to write a summary of information.

Purpose: To exercise comprehensive thinking skills.

Summarizing automatically calls forth thinking. It is not possible to summarize something effectively without considering the whole of it, sorting out its significant and insignificant elements. Use your imagination in asking students to summarize. Here are some ideas:

- Ask students to write the theme of a story in less than 30 words.
- Ask students to summarize the work of Edison in less than 50 words.
- Ask students to draw a sketch showing how something works.
- Ask students to outline the arguments for and against slavery in 1850.
- Ask students to identify the main ideas covered so far.
- Ask students to summarize what they've learned so far during a certain unit.

Strategy 13.6: Make a Prediction

Description: Asking students to think ahead and make predictions.

Purpose: To exercise the ability to think ahead.

This is a fairly straightforward strategy. Simply ask students to predict something. For instance: the approximate answer to a math problem, what a chapter in a novel is about, how the film will end, what Edison did when he kept failing.

You might also ask students to note more than one possible outcome and then rank each in terms of likelihood and, perhaps, personal preference:

- We talked about several ways of . . . (increasing awareness of world events, insulating old homes in town, changing the class seating arrangement, publishing a class newsletter, etc.). Which would you say has the best chance of working? Next best chance? Please list the ways we discussed in the order of your personal preference.

• Consider what might happen if . . . (the United Nations had the only world police force, no candy was allowed in school, we all wrote our personal letters in poetry, etc.). List the possible consequences of such an act. Then number them in order, from the most likely to the least likely to occur. Finally, star the two consequences you personally would most prefer, even if they are not very likely.

Strategy 13.7: What Might Explain? —————————

Description: Asking students to consider what might explain an event.

Purpose: To exercise cause-and-effect thinking.

Ask students, "What happened before?" or "What might explain this event?" The intent here is to motivate students to think about relationships between causes and effects. For example:

• What factors might have contributed to the water boiling in that situation?

• What factors might have contributed to World War II?

• What factors might have contributed to our crowded highways?

• What factors might have contributed to Mark Twain's popularity as a writer?

Many explanations are incomplete. We often do not know all of what caused something. What led to the water boiling? Correct, although incomplete, answers might include "the heat under the pot," "enough time for the heat to raise the water temperature," "my intention to boil water," or "the absence of ice being added to the water."

The best answer to "why" questions is often "I'm not entirely sure, but I would include these main factors. . . . " For that reason, asking "why" invites careless thinking. It invites students to conclude that events can be explained fully. That is rarely true. It is not a conclusion I want my students to carry into life. I prefer they keep open to new and more complete explanations.

For that reason, I recommend not asking simple "why" questions but instead using a more open-ended question form, such as: Can you think of reasons why . . .? What are some of the factors that might explain . . .? Do you have any explanations for . . .? Why would you say . . .? Can you identify some of the main reasons for . . .? What might explain . . .? See if you can discover why. . . .

Strategy 13.8: Solve a Problem

Description: Asking students to solve a problem that lacks an obvious solution.

Purpose: To exercise problem-solving skills.

You can vary the difficulty of problems by giving students more or less of the data needed to solve the problems. Here are some examples:

• List the eating needs of three different dogs and the costs and nutritional values of four different dog foods. The question: What would be a good plan for feeding the dogs at a cost of less than $100 a month? If you have reasons for your choices, tell what they are.

• Supply information about a person, real or fictional, who is trying to accomplish something (e.g., get a job, save money, eat a healthy breakfast, stop smoking, etc.). The key question: What else would you want to know before recommending a plan to this person? What plan would you recommend? What problems do you predict might complicate your plan?

• Pick a real-life problem to solve: What might be a better way to distribute books in class? What might be a better way to take attendance? How can we better keep work groups from losing track of time? How can we deal with the poverty in town? What should we do about traffic congestion on Main Street? What can you do to stop yourself from watching too much television?

Strategy 13.9: Brainstorm Alternatives

Description: A group thinks open-mindedly about a topic and generates a written list of possibilities without worrying whether any possibility is reasonable.

Purpose: To exercise creative thinking skills.

This strategy can be used in small or large groups. Tell students you want them to create the largest possible list of alternatives for accomplishing a specific task, such as balancing a budget, choosing a story topic, finding an effective way to read a chapter, doing mental long division, heating a home, or reducing violence.

Provide students with three useful guidelines for brainstorming in small groups:

• Accept all ideas without judgment. One unrealistic idea may generate a new valuable idea.

• Write all ideas as they are mentioned. Do not attempt to judge each idea as it is offered. Keep minds open during the brainstorming. Judgments are for later, when you look back over your written list.

• Generate ideas quickly. High energy and quick pace often lead to new creativity. If ideas come too fast for one person to write them, get two or more to take turns recording what's said.

14 Strategies for Teaching Beyond Facts and Details

Isolated facts and details often have limited value. To become truly meaningful, they must be woven into a larger context. The strategies in this chapter are designed to help you weave together four subject matter levels: (1) facts and details, (2) concepts and generalizations, (3) applications, and (4) personal values, defined as follows:

1. Facts and details. Specific pieces of information, such as names, dates, individual events, or facts with limited usefulness by themselves.

• On what date was the Declaration of Independence signed? Where was it signed?
• What is the chemical symbol for water? For sodium chloride?
• What reason did the main character give for hiding his gun? Where did he hide it?
• What were the four main causes of World War II? Who were our allies?
• What is 23 x 145?

2. Concepts and generalizations. Broad truths or ideas or skills generally useful.

• What motivates people to declare their independence? What is a declaration?
• How are elements joined into chemical wholes? How are symbols derived?

• How are violent acts related to frustration? What often leads to violence?

• What forces contribute to warfare? To international cooperation?

• What's an efficient way to get a total from a group of identical amounts?

3. Applications. Practical uses of knowledge or skills:

• What people in the world today want more independence? What are they doing to try to achieve it?

• How would you analyze this sample? What pollutes the air in our town?

• What kinds of violence are increasing these days? What might cause these increases?

• What kinds of conflicts do we find in our town? What might explain these conflicts?

• How many total square inches are contained in all our desk tops put together?

4. Personal values. Principles, consciously or unconsciously held, that affect one's personal behavior.

• What would motivate you to act independently of a group? When have you done that?

• What are the most important parts of your life? Do you have symbols you very much care about?

• How do you handle frustration? What would help you better handle frustration?

• Are there any conflicts now that bother you? Is there more you can do about any of them?

• Can you recall occasions when you would have liked to be able to do multiplication quickly or easily? Would you like any help with multiplication?

Each level of subject matter makes a unique contribution to the whole of learning. The strategies in this chapter suggest how you can take advantage of these levels in your teaching.

Strategy 14.1: Concept/Generalization Focus

Description: A lesson or unit built around a concept or generalization, not a set of facts.

Purpose: To bring student learning up to the level of concepts and generalizations.

We can center a unit around a big idea, such as a concept or generalization. In science, for example, we can center a unit on balance, evaporation, or plant growth. In art, on color, movement, or sketching. In English, on poetry, metaphor, or comedy. With this strategy, we use facts and details to illuminate the big ideas or general skills. As a result, many students remember the facts. They pick them up in passing, much as we learn the names of the streets in our neighborhood by passing them repeatedly. Here are some examples of how this strategy might be used in different subjects:

Geography. "Today we will start a unit on Europe. We'll occasionally use flash cards to help you connect cities with their countries. We'll see a film on the rivers and mountains of Europe. We'll read about people from different regions. And I'll ask you each to draw a map that shows the location of everything we study. The map will make you pay attention to a lot of facts and details. Some of the facts will stick in your memory, but there is no need to remember any particular fact. Aim to get the *idea* of Europe as a region, such as where it is, what it looks like, what it's people are about. As we proceed, please make a list of interesting things you learned. At the end of the unit, I'll ask you to turn in your map and summarize your list of learnings, so I know the main things you learned about Europe and, perhaps, what interested or surprised you most."

Mathematics. "Today we will start a unit on percentages. Your job is to prepare a scrapbook of several kinds of percentage problems, showing how you can correctly solve each one. This will require you to understand where percentage problems are used in real life. And you will have to figure out a way to solve such problems correctly. We'll explore all that and help each other. Many of you will master the process of doing percentage calculations during this unit. But the process might still be tricky for some of you, so don't worry if your time for mastering the calculations has not yet arrived. Practice asking someone to help you solve your problems correctly. But be sure your scrapbook shows you can identify several kinds of percentage problems and, by yourself or with help, get each correctly solved."

History. "We will begin our unit on the Civil War. Our approach will be to look closely at the daily lives of six people who lived during that time, some famous and some not. As we do this, you will pick up many details and facts about the war and about life during that time. Some of you will remember the facts, but I would not like you to aim for that. Aim rather to get a general understanding of the war, and especially of how people on different sides of the issue experienced it.

"At the end of the unit, I'll give you some time to work with one or two others, or alone if you like, to prepare a written or oral report, or perhaps a mural, dramatic skit, or model. Your task for this final work is to show some of the key things you learned about the Civil War."

Concluding questions or summary evaluations would not, of course, focus on the facts of the lessons. Instead, they would focus on the big picture. For instance:

• "What in general can you say about . . . the three chemicals we studied so far . . . the misspelled words on the board . . . the stories we read . . . how plants grow . . . the American history leaders we discussed?"

• "Classify the specifics we studied into the concepts of . . . organic and inorganic chemicals . . . spelling exceptions and nonexceptions . . . subjective and objective writing . . . the plant-growth factors of soil, light, temperature . . . favoring democracy and not favoring democracy."

• "Write some outcome sentences about the lesson beginning with such phrases as I learned, I was surprised, I'm beginning to wonder, I promise, or I believe."

• "Compare and contrast . . . the three chemicals we studied with chemicals we studied before . . . subjective and objective writing . . . early and late plant growth . . . Lincoln and Lee. Identify some things that are the same and some that are different."

Many students come to realize that they forget many facts soon after the final exam and that even if they remember all the facts, the facts themselves are often not very useful other than for winning trivia games, perhaps. Yet many students *assume* that memorizing facts is what school is all about. For this reason, it is often prudent to explain clearly that you want students to clarify a larger issue, or advance a general skill, or grasp a basic concept, and not merely to remember a batch of details. Telling students up front that this is your focus helps many let go of limiting assumptions about what they might gain from school.

Strategy 14.2: Connecting Subject Matter to Values ———

Description: A lesson or unit connecting an academic topic to an issue students personally care about.

Purpose: To encourage students to exercise mature thinking on real-life issues and to motivate academic study.

———

Often it is possible to begin a unit with a values-level discussion, more particularly, a discussion about an issue that students care about. Alternatively, the class may end with such a discussion. Here are some examples of this strategy at work:

Example 1. The teacher picks a concept from a book the class has been studying and starts the lesson with values-level questions likely to touch student concerns or interests: "One theme in the book we just finished was perseverance, not giving up even when the going got tough. Make some notes to yourself about times when you or someone you know stuck to a task, even when that was very difficult. Then, thinking about your examples, note anything that made persevering easier. What ideas does our story suggest about perseverance that might be useful for you to remember?"

Example 2. The teacher picks a concept related to a historical event or famous person and connects it to value issues that concern students, using it either before or after study.

Before Study: "Lincoln was sometimes unsure of what he should do as President of the United States, as our next unit will make clear. How about you? Can you identify times when you remember being unsure of what to do? What's a good strategy for handling times like that? Let's think about this a bit now and then again after we study our unit, to see if we learn anything more about making choices when we are unsure.

I will add my thoughts, too. People often must choose, even when they are not sure what the best choice is. In this unit, one of the things I want you to learn is something about how to make choices wisely."

After Study: "As we learned, Alaska and Hawaii were the last states to be admitted to the United States, yet most of the people in Alaska and Hawaii were not unhappy about being last. How about you? Were you ever last or almost last at something? How did you feel? What would make being last okay? What makes it harder when you are not among the first few to do something?"

Example 3. Connecting mathematics to reality can effectively motivate new study or add a dimension of meaning to completed study.

New Study: "Before we move ahead with subtraction of large numbers, I want each of you to collect three examples of subtraction from real life. Use your imagination or ask family members for some ideas. Then consider what would be very hard for you to subtract from your life and what you would love to get rid of."

Completed Study: "Before going on to our next unit in geometry, let's spend a few minutes talking about circles in the real world. We'll share ideas later, first in pairs and then as a whole class, but first make some notes about one or more of the questions I wrote on the board. What circles of things or people or ideas are important to you? What feelings, if any, have you about circles? Have you any broken circles in your life? Are there any circles you could complete for others? Can you draw a silly circle?

Steps for Building a Values Discussion

1. Seek a concept or application related to the unit that might touch students' personal lives. For instance:

prejudice	money	luxuries
honesty	special people	blind people
things I love to do	giving up	favorite games
hope	stealing	winning
generosity	dying	strong personal beliefs
understanding	delight	fear
deception	courage	loneliness
cars	fury	perseverance
great surprise	helping strangers	jealousy

sorrow	telling the truth	crime in town
giving compliments	kindness	the way you look
insecurity	planning ahead	disappointment
love	keeping a secret	friends
teasing	hugging	smiles
pets	bossiness	cruelty
the years ahead	hobbies	being too short
strong feelings	tears and laughter	a gift
gifts	terrible mistake	hopes for the future

2. Ask questions in which the word "you" is predominant. For example:

- Have you ever experienced something like . . . ?
- Do you know someone who . . . ?
- Have you ever enjoyed . . . ?
- Have you ever had trouble with . . . ?
- What might you do if . . . ?
- What else might you do?
- What choice would make you feel best about yourself?
- What would you most want to avoid doing?

3. Structure a safe, thoughtful way to handle the values considerations. I often use the Write-Share-Learn lesson plan on page 12. And I typically offer students the option to pass on any question or any procedure, which allows them to protect their privacy if they wish and to practice managing their options.

Some Comments on Values and Subject Matter

Values-level considerations used either before or after the study of facts, concepts, and applications not only can spark students' interest but can give students practice in thinking seriously about important life issues, practice that many students sorely need. Young people will face many complex choices in their life. They will face those choices with more balance and reason, and far less instability and impulse, when they have the opportunity to grapple with issues in the safety of the classroom.

When taking a unit to the values level of subject matter, I find little need to make the leap logical. For instance, with the concept of circles, one can leap from circles in geometry to circles of friends or circles of personal habits. With the concept of rocks, one can leap from categorizing hard rocks to wondering about hard people and how best to deal with them. With the concept of long division, one can leap to divisions in our personal lives or in the school or community. Here are some examples:

Example 1. "Now that we have looked at the geography of the earth's crust, I'd like to take a few minutes to look at how people from different lands relate, or how people within one land relate when they are different from one another. Please make a note or two about how you feel when you meet someone from a foreign land or someone who is very different from you. You don't need to share your notes with anyone; keep them private if you like." Students write for a minute or two, then the teacher might say, "Sit with someone near you and share only those thoughts that you want to share. Just a moment or so for this." After a few moments, the teacher might say, "Let's all discuss how we want to feel or act with people who are different from us."

Example 2. "Now that we have finished our unit on percentages, I'd like to take a few minutes to talk about percentages in your personal life. Please start by writing down an estimate of the percentage of time over the past two weeks that you've felt strong, capable, confident. Then write down what you might do to increase that percentage, if you have any ideas about that. I'll give you just a moment or two to make some notes. Then you'll have a chance to share thoughts with a partner and, finally, we'll all get back together and I'll give you some of my ideas for being strong, capable, and confident more of the time."

Example 3. "Before we leave the Civil War unit, let's see if we can list on the chalkboard some ideas for talking over conflicts peaceably, resolving differences before they get into negative, hard feelings. Let's say two friends are in conflict. What kind of conflict might that be? What are some smart and not so smart ways to resolve such a conflict? . . . "

Such leaps allows us to create powerful lessons, teach students about what is involved in good living, and keep schoolwork filled with rich variety. Many students learn as much from personal values discussions as from academic studies.

Teachers sometimes assume they should begin lessons at the fact-detail level—for instance, teaching relevant names and dates in history before studying what actually happened, learning grammar and spelling before writing letters, learning the parts of the microscope before beginning to use it. There is logic in the argument, but a logic that often squeezes much of the life out of teaching.

Strategy 14.3: Application Projects

Description: Projects in which students apply what they have learned to real-life situations.

Purpose: To make learning more meaningful to students.

We can often move subject matter to the application level simply by asking students to take something they've learned and find ways to apply it in real life.

Example 1. Students have just learned that 8 x 3 = 24. The teacher asks for a possible real-life application of this problem. One student says, "Well, if there were three families and eight people in each family, that would be an example."

"Yes, that would fit," the teacher says. "Who has another idea?"

Another student answers, "How about three pizzas, each with eight slices?"

"Yes," says the teacher, "8 x 3 would tell us how many slices all together. Who else would risk sharing a possible application for 8 x 3?"

Example 2. Students have been studying the Bill of Rights. The teacher says, "Take a few moments and jot down one or two rights you think are not very well protected in our community. Perhaps also try to write some words for a law that would better protect those rights."

After a few students have finished writing, the teacher announces, "One minute more." Then she asks students to use the Sharing Pairs strategy to briefly compare notes. She follows this activity with whole-class discussion of some of the students' ideas. The teacher concludes the discussion by inviting students to propose some new laws to protect people's rights.

Example 3. A teacher talks to the class about the wisdom of thinking before acting. Then she says to the class, "Write some notes as you think about these questions: Is there someone in your life, perhaps a friend or relative, who you wish would do more thinking before acting? Or are there some situations outside of school in which you yourself might do more thinking before acting?"

After students have been writing for a few minutes, the teacher says, "You can keep any of your responses to these questions private, but I was wondering if anyone would like to share some of their responses."

Several students do volunteer, and a brief discussion follows. The teacher concludes the discussion by saying, "In all of life, now and later, perhaps especially when you are out of school, there are advantages in pausing to think before you act. You may want to practice building that habit into your life. If you find a good way to practice doing this, let the rest of us know about it sometime, perhaps when I ask what is new or good in your life, as I sometimes do at the beginning of a class. I think we all enjoy hearing how each of us is doing something to make our life a little bit better."

Example 4. After completing a unit, the teacher says, "Think back to something you've learned during this unit. Can you imagine a practical use for what you learned? I want you to write or draw something that tells what uses you've thought of. Work alone or with one or two partners. Tomorrow we will share our ideas."

When students are regularly asked to apply what they have learned to the real world, they get into the habit of connecting learning with living, and they become better at both.

Strategy 14.4: What I Know, What I Want to Know (or K-W-L)

Description: In preparation for study, asking students to note what they already know about a topic and what they might want to know about it.

Purpose: To build a unit on the knowledge and questions students bring to it.

I do not recall my teachers ever asking me what I wanted to learn when I was a student. If I has been asked, I might have thought about it and uncovered a curiosity or two. And if I heard my classmates' curiosities, I likely would have discovered even more I wanted to learn. As it was, my classmates and I most of the time sat quite passively through our lessons, taking what we got, like it or not, with most of our curiosities gradually drying up.

For many years, I've found it valuable to ask my students what they know about a topic and what they want to know. Donna Ogle (1986; Carr and Ogle 1987) advocates much the same approach in what she calls the K-W-L strategy: K = what I know; W = what I want to know; L = what I learned. Here's an example of how this strategy works:

> "We will begin a unit on the United States Congress today. What are some things you already know about Congress? Let's brainstorm. I'd like two newsprint writers to come up and take turns writing down all the ideas that come up. Who will start us off? We want a list of things you already know about Congress."

Once students have listed most of their ideas and seem ready to move on, the teacher continues:

> "We'll leave that list posted for a while. Now let's start another list. What are some things you would *like* to know about Congress? What are some things you are curious about or concerned about? Be creative and open-minded. Who will start our brainstorming?"

If the teacher suspects students will produce a thin list on their own, the pump could be primed with some comments:

> "For example, you may wonder how to meet with your representative. Or how you can *become* one. Or how much it costs to get elected. Or you may wonder if representatives really read citizens' letters. Of if it makes any difference. Or why we have so many representatives in congress. Or about scandals. Or what people think of the present congress and what congress should do. Do any of those questions interest anyone here?"

The particular questions students list at the outset do not limit the learnings that will eventually result. A teacher can add any content deemed appropriate. The list of what students want to know is simply a starting point to open minds to the unit. Once the lists have been completed, a teacher has several options:

Option 1: Leave the lists posted for future reference. Simply proceed with instruction as usual, taking advantage of the fact that students will now probably be more motivated to dig into the unit, looking forward to uncovering some of the things they want to know. The teacher also has the advantage of knowing what the class already knows and what interests them, which will probably help her better plan instruction.

At the end of the unit, the teacher might say, "Looking back on our study, I'd like you to take some time to review what you've learned. First, make a list of your key learnings. Then compare your list with the lists we made the first day and note answers to these questions: (1) Did you learn that something you originally thought was true was not exactly as you first understood it? (2) Did you learn anything very new? (3) What now would you say are the three or four most important things you know about the United States Congress? (4) Do you now have some questions you still wonder about? We'll share answers in pairs and then use a Whip Around to sample the whole group's ideas."

Option 2: Update the lists as the unit proceeds. The teacher works with students to gradually revise and augment the lists so, at the end of the unit, they represent what is then known and what is yet of interest to students. One teacher I know told me that a 4th grade class in his school formed a committee to reproduce the two lists in typed form and then gave them to students to take home so they could show their families what they've been learning.

Option 3: Turn the lists into cooperative learning activities. Students who have similar interests can get together and study further, using a convenient form of cooperative learning or, in the words of Yael and Schlomo Sharan (1989/1990), the "group investigation model." Here's how a teacher might introduce this idea: "I'd like you to design your own study now, based on what interests you. Although you may work alone, I'd prefer that you work with one or two of your classmates. And I prefer that no group have more than three members because it's hard for everyone to keep active and involved when there are four or more people in one group. Let's see if we have any common interests. Who can say what they would like to investigate? Speak up if you have an idea and then we'll see who might be interested in that same general idea."

Alternatively, a teacher could create a chart on which students sign up for topics or could arbitrarily assign students to trios, as by having a class of thirty count off by tens. Or a teacher could announce: "I'd like you to get into trios now, sitting with people with whom you have not worked recently. Get to know some new friends better." Once groups are set: "Now, before I tell you about deadlines and what product I'd like each group to produce, I'd like you to talk over some possibilities for your group investigation. What might be fun or important to do or learn more about?"

Used with appropriate topics, this strategy usually leads to rich learning experiences. When students participate in shaping the focus of study, often their dignity flowers, the class energy level goes up, self-management comes alive, community feelings grow, and awareness sharpens.

Strategy 14.5: Concept Chart

Description: A classroom chart of important concepts studied, posted, and reviewed to deepen appreciation of those concepts.

Purpose: To keep key concepts fresh and alive in students' minds.

Imagine walking into a classroom and seeing a newsprint sheet on the wall listing the following:

- friendship
- courage
- equality of opportunity
- loyalty
- kindness
- self-control of impulses
- integrity
- whole self
- striving and accepting
- candor
- supportive behavior
- intrusive behavior

You ask about it and the teacher explains, "I call that a concept chart. Whenever an important idea comes up in class I write it on that chart. I refer back to those ideas from time to time, when they naturally come up in class. I sometimes include important names, even symbols I want students to remember. But mainly I include concepts I want students to internalize that are unlikely to be completely understood the first time they come up in lessons. It helps me keep key ideas fresh and active." The Concept Chart strategy is as simple as that.

About the Author

Merrill Harmin is a Professor of Education at Southern Illinois University, Edwardsville. He received his Ph.D. from New York University in 1960 and has since published numerous books and articles, including *How to Plan a Program for Moral Education*, which is part of ASCD's series of How-To books. He is the Director of the Inspiration Strategies Institute, a research-training organization that focuses on inspirational ways to do the jobs we have to do.

Acknowledgments

No author produces a book alone. I had help from many people. Kelly Shull coordinated the gathering of the strategies for the book, and Amy Hansen, Beth Brukemper, Cathy McGarrahan, Kathy Long, Meg Dees, Patrice Bain, Tracy Ziemba-Winslade, and Yvonne Mitkos made very special contributions to it.

Few of the strategies in this book come from any one source. Most have grown out of the experiences, creativity, and goodwill of many professionals, some of whose names appear below and others whose names appear in the Recommended Readings. My role in this endeavor consisted largely of giving names to what teachers told me worked and then asking other teachers with whom I have worked over the years if the same or similar strategies have worked for them. This book is truly a collection of ideas. I thank the following people for so graciously shaping and testing the strategies in this book:

Andy LePage, Ann Lowe, Anne Bailey, Anne Hyman, Anne Marie McMahon, Barbara Goldenhersh, Barbara Saul, Barbara Thielmann, Besse Dale, Betty Hatch, Beverly Douglas, Bill Gallagher, Bill Greive, Bill Shuey, Bob Reasoner, Bruce Maskow, Candi Cangelosi-Johnson, Carol Kreitner, Carol Norris, Carol Smalley, Catherine McGarrahan, Cathy Anise, Cathy Bay, Celeste Williams, Charles Pearson, Cheryl Greaves, Connie Dembrowsky, Crystal Lawler, Cynthia Hussain, Dale Paulus, Darlene McDaniel, Dave Thornburg, Dave Valley, Debbie Mansin, Dennis Butts, Diana Taylor, Diane Frey, Diane Highlander, Donald Baden, Donald Keefe, Dov Elkins, Elena Wallace, Elizabeth Hall, Esther Wright, Florence Horne, Florine Epplin, Gail Dusa, Gary Nunn, Gary Swalley, Gene Bedley, Guy Sachs, Hanoch McCarty, Hayman Kite, Helen Mings, Herschel Prater, Howard Kirshenbaum, Jack Canfield, Jack Schlueter, Jackie Bennett, Jacqueline Riggs, James Andris, James Comer, James Owens, Jan Scanlan, Jane

Gregg, Jane Heitzig, Jane Holcomb, Jane Van Vertloo, Janet McCann, Janice Hapgood, Jean Kauffmann, Jean Peek, Jeanette Tremoulet, Jeanne Swain, Jeffrey Boyles, Jill Schwear, Joe Munshaw, John Hart, John Prieskorn, John Vasconcellos, Joseph Webber, Judith Albracht, Judy Kupsky, Julie Corey, Julie Evans, Julie Wilcox, Karen Eastby, Karen Gitcho, Karen Herrington, Karen Rains, Kathleen Gallagher, Kathy Matthews, Kathy Mayr, Kathy Smith, Ken Miller, Lana Rogier, Larry Hopp, Laurie Malone, Lawrence Kolhberg, Lellie Bryant, LeRoy Foster, Leslie Wehling, Linda Sauerwein, Linda Zoll, Linda Zorger, Lois Adomite, Lou Obernuefemann, Louis Raths, Lovann Brown, Lynn Fox, Maralee Rivard, Margaret Grueter, Marie Hackett, Marilyn Brown, Marilyn Taylor, Marva Collins, Marvin Cohn, Mary Anne Dalton, Mary Jane Ostanik, Mary Rader, Melita Bearinger, Michele Borba, Michele Morgan, Miriam Harmon, Chick Moorman, Nancy Moorman, Nathan Swift, Peggy Bielen, Penny Kennedy, Peter Pierro, Phillip Besonen, Ray Grinter, Rich Revheim, Richard Tempko, Rick Galinas, Robert Rockwell, Robert Russo, Robert Shaw, Robert Williams, Ruth Ambruster, Saville Sax, Sherry Wimmer, Sidney Simon, Stacey Lynn, Sue Burke, Sue Underwood, Susan Nall, Thomas O'Brien, Trudie Hotson, Valerie Meyer, Vicky Summers, Wanda East, William Conway, Yolander Williams, Yvonne Broger, Yvonne Halvachs

Three sources call for special acknowledgment. First, John Dewey, from whom I first learned that good learning and good living should and can be cultivated together. He is also the chief source for several of the strategies dealing with class climate and student project work, and for a good deal of the spirit pervading other strategies as well.

Then there is Louis Raths, my mentor in graduate school. He showed me practical ways to nurture the hidden potential in all students. He is also one of the sources for strategies dealing with subject matter selection, thinking questions, and ways to respond to students that go well beyond praise and rewards.

And, finally, I thank Grace Pilon, the creator of WORKSHOP WAY.® Pilon has designed a comprehensive K-12 classroom instructional system that *always* serves DESCA, even with the driest of academic content and the most antagonistic of students. Furthermore, her system is sufficiently detailed and workable so even burned-out teachers are able to get it to work. You may want to do what I did: observe some of the teachers around the country using Pilon's design. You'll find dramatic demonstrations of what the profession now knows about teaching methodology. To identify teachers using WORKSHOP WAY or to obtain Pilon's publications, contact: The Workshop Way, Inc., P.O. Box 850170, New Orleans, LA 70185-0170.

References and Recommended Resources

Introduction

Anderson, L. W., and J. C. Anderson. (April 1982). "Affective Assessment Is Necessary and Possible." *Educational Leadership* 39, 7: 524-525.

Anderson, R., E. Hiebert, J. Scott, and I. Wilkinson. (1985). *Becoming a Nation of Readers: A Report of the Commission on Reading.* Washington, D.C.: National Institute of Education.

Ashton, P. T., and R. B. Webb. (1986). *Making a Difference: Teachers' Sense of Efficacy and Student Achievement.* New York: Longman.

Bloom, B. S. (1976). *Human Characteristics and School Learning.* New York: McGraw-Hill.

Bredderman, T. (1983). "The Effects of Activity-Based Elementary Science on Student Outcomes: A Quantitative Synthesis." *Review of Educational Research.* 54: 499-518.

Carter, K. (1990). "Teacher's Knowledge and Learning to Teach." In *Handbook of Research on Teacher Education,* edited by R. Houston. New York: Macmillan.

Dewey, J. (1916). *Democracy and Education.* New York: Macmillan.

Dewey, J. (1938). *Experience and Education.* New York: Macmillan.

Dillon-Peterson, B. (1986). "Trusting Teachers to Know What Is Good for Them." In *Improving Teaching,* edited by K. Zumwalt. Alexandria, Va.: ASCD.

Donmoyer, R. (1985). "The Rescue from Relativism: Two Failed Attempts and an Alternative Strategy." *Educational Researcher* 14, 10: 13-20.

Frick, W. R. (1981). *Humanistic Psychology: Conversations with Abraham Maslow, Gardner Murphy and Carl Rogers.* Bristol, Ind.: Wyndham Hall Press.

Good, T., and J. Brophy. (1990). *Educational Psychology: A Realistic Approach.* New York: Longman.

Goodlad, J. (1984). *A Place Called School.* New York: McGraw-Hill.

Guilford, J. (1967). *The Nature of Human Intelligence.* New York: McGraw-Hill.

Habermas, J. (1971). *Knowledge and Human Interests,* translated by J. Shapiro. Boston: Beacon Press.

Henson, K. (1988). *Methods and Strategies for Teaching in Secondary and Middle Schools.* New York: Longman.

Hughes, A. L., and K. Frommer. (April 1982). "A System for Monitoring Affective Objectives." *Educational Leadership* 39, 7: 521-523.

James, W. (1980). *Principles of Psychology.* Mineola, N.Y.: Dover.

Jourard, S. (1980). *Healthy Personality: An Approach from the Point of View of Humanistic Psychology.* Riverside: Macmillan.

Joyce, B., and M. Weil. (1980). *Models of Teaching.* 2nd ed. Englewood Cliffs, N.J.: Prentice-Hall.

McLeish, J. (1976). "Lecture Method." In *The Psychology of Teaching Methods, Part I* (75th Yearbook of the National Society for the Study of Education), edited by N. L. Gage. Chicago: University of Chicago.

McLuhan, M., and Q. Fiore. (1967). *The Medium Is the Message.* New York: Bantam.

Maslow, A. (1968). *Toward a Psychology of Being.* New York: Reinhold.

Miller, J. P, B. Cassie, and S. Drake. (1991). *Holistic Learning: A Teacher's Guide to Integrated Studies.* Toronto: OISE Press.

National Commission on Excellence in Education. (1983). *A Nation at Risk: The Imperative for Educational Reform.* Washington, D.C.: Government Printing Office.

Novak, F. (1993). "Advancing Invitational Thinking." *Great Ideas in Education* 1: 19.

Pederson, E., T. A. Faucher, and W. W. Eaton. (February 1978). "A New Perspective on the Effects of First-Grade Teachers on Children's Subsequent Adult Status." *Harvard Educational Review* 48, 1: 1-31.

Piaget, J. (1983). "Piaget's Theory." In *Handbook of Child Psychology,* edited by J. H. Flavell and A. M. Markman. New York: Wiley.

Pilon, G. H. (1981). *Workshop Way in High School*. New Orleans, La.: Workshop Way, Inc.

Pilon, G. H. (1987). *Workshop Way Practical Handbook*. (Grades 2-8). New Orleans, La.: Workshop Way, Inc.

Pilon, G. H. (1991). *Workshop Way*. New Orleans, La.: Workshop Way, Inc.

Popper, K. R. (1959). *The Logic of Scientific Discovery*. New York: Harper & Row.

Richards, J. (1982). "Homework." In *Encyclopedias of Educational Research*, 5th ed., edited by H. Mitzel. New York: Macmillan.

Rosenholtz, S. (1989). *Teacher's Workplace: The Social Organization of Schools*. New York: Longman.

Rosenshine, B. (December 1968). "To Explain: A Review of Research." *Educational Leadership* 26, 3: 303-309.

Rosenshine, B. (1983). "Teaching Functions in Instructional Programs." *The Elementary School Journal* 83: 335-351.

Sylwester, R., and J. Y. Choo. (December 1992). "What Brain Research Says About Paying Attention." *Educational Leadership* 50, 4: 71-77.

Tyler, R. (1950). *Basic Principles of Curriculum and Instruction*. Chicago: University of Chicago.

Zumwalt, K., editor (1986). *Improving Teaching*. Alexandria, Va.: ASCD.

Instructing (Chapters 1 and 2)

Annis, L. (1983). "The Processes and Effects of Peer Tutoring." *Human Learning* 2: 39-47.

American Association for the Advancement of Science. (1970). *Science: A Process Approach*. New York: Xerox Education Division.

Baumann, J. F. (1992). "Effect of Think-Aloud Instruction on Elementary Students' Comprehension Monitoring Abilities." *Journal of Reading Behavior* 24, 2: 143-172.

Bellanca, J., and R. Fogarty. (1990). *Blueprints for Cooperative Learning in the Thinking Classroom*. Palatine, Ill.: Skylight.

Beyer, B. K. (1982). "Using Writing to Learn Social Studies." *The Social Studies* 18: 100-105.

Brandt, R., ed. (1989). *Readings from Educational Leadership: Teaching Thinking*. Alexandria, Va.: ASCD.

Bruner, J., J. J. Goodnow, and G. Austin. (1956). *A Study of Thinking*. New York: Wiley.

Clegg, A. A., Jr. (1971). "Classroom Questions." In *The Encyclopedia of Education*, Vol. 2. (pp. 2, 183-190). New York: Macmillan.

Costa, A., and L. Lowrey. (1989). *Techniques for Teaching Thinking*. Pacific Grove, Calif.: Midwest Publications.

Crump, C. (April 1970). "Teachers, Questions, and Cognition." *Educational Leadership* 27, 7: 657-660.

Cummings, C. (1980). *Teaching Makes a Difference*. Edmonds, Wash.: Teaching Inc.

Davis, O.L., Jr., and F. P. Hunkins. (1966). "Textbook Questions: What Thinking Processes Do They Foster?" *Peabody Journal of Education* 43: 285-292.

Dillon, J. T. (November 1984). "Research on Questioning and Discussion." *Educational Leadership* 42, 3: 50-56.

Dillon, J. T. (1988). *Questioning and Teaching*. New York: Teachers College Press.

Dreyfus, A., and R. Lieberman. (Summer 1981). "Perceptions, Expectations and Interactions: The Essential Ingredients for a Genuine Classroom Discussion." *Journal of Biological Education* 15, 2: 153-157.

Gabbert, B., D. W. Johnson, and R. Johnson. (1986). "Cooperative Learning, Group-to-Individual Transfer, Process Gain, and the Acquisition of Cognitive Reasoning Strategies." *Journal of Psychology* 120: 265-278.

Gall, M. (December 1970). "The Use of Questions in Teaching." *Review of Educational Research* 40, 5: 207-220.

Hartford, F. (October 1982). "Training Chemistry Students to Ask Research Question."

Journal of Research in Science Teaching 19, 7: 559-570.

Howell, W. S., and D. K. Smith. (1956). *Discussion* (pp. 36-37). New York: Macmillan.

Hunter, M. C., (1976). *Rx: Improved Instruction*. El Segundo, Calif.: T.I.P. Publications.

Hunter, M. (September 1979a). "Diagnostic Teaching" *The Elementary School Journal* 80: 41-46.

Hunter, M. (October 1979b). "Teaching Is Decision Making." *Educational Leadership* 37, 1: 62-67.

Hunter, M. (1984). "Knowing, Teaching, and Supervising." In *Using What We Know About Teaching*, edited by P. Hosford (1984 Yearbook). Alexandria, Va.: ASCD.

Johnson, D. W., and R. Johnson. (1987). *Creative Conflict*. Edina, Minn.: Interaction Book Company.

Johnson, D. W., and R. Johnson. (1989). *Cooperation and Competition: Theory and Research*. Edina, Minn.: Interaction Book Company.

Jones, B. F., M. R. Amiran, and M. Katims. (1985). "Teaching Cognitive Strategies and Text Structures." *Thinking and Learning Skills: Relating Instruction to Research. Vol. 1*, edited by J. Segal, S. F. Chipman, and R. Glaser. Hillsdale, N.J.: Lawrence Erlbaum.

Jones, B. F., A. S. Palincsar, D. S. Ogle, and E. G. Carr, eds. (1987). *Strategic Teaching and Learning: Cognitive Instruction in the Content Areas*. Alexandria, Va.: ASCD.

Joyce, B., and M. Weil. (1991). *Models of Teaching*. Englewood Cliffs, N.J.: Prentice-Hall.

McTighe, J., and F. T. Lyman, Jr. (April 1988). "Cueing Thinking in the Classroom: The Promise of Theory-Embedded Tools." *Educational Leadership* 45, 7: 18-24.

Mills, S., C. Rice, D. Berliner, and E. Rosseau. (Spring 1980). "The Correspondence Between Teacher Questions and Student Answers in Classroom Discourse." *Journal of Experimental Education* 48, 3: 194-204.

Padilla, M., J. Okey, and G. Dilshaw. (March 1983). "The Relationship Between Science Process Skill and Formal Thinking Abilities." *Journal of Research in Science Teaching* 20, 3: 239-246.

Palincsar, A. S. (October 1986). "Metacognitive Strategy Instruction." *Exceptional Children* 53, 2: 118-124.

Palincsar, A. S., and D. A. Brown. (February 1987). "Enhancing Instructional Time Through Attention to Metacognition." *Journal of Learning Disabilities* 20, 2: 66-75.

Redfield, D., and E. Rousseau. (Summer 1981). "A Meta-Analysis on Teacher Questioning Behavior." *Review of Educational Research* 51: 234-245.

Riley, J. (1980). *The Effects of Teachers' Wait-time and Cognitive Questioning Level on Pupil Science Development*. Paper presented at the Annual Meeting of the National Association for Research in Science Teaching, Boston.

Rosenshine, B. (1976). "Classroom Instruction." In *Psychology of Teaching: The 77th Yearbook of the National Study of Education*, edited by N. Gage. Chicago: University of Chicago Press.

Rosenshine, B. (1979). "Content, Time and Direct Instruction." *Research on Teaching*, edited by P. L. Peterson and H. J. Walberg. Berkeley: McCutchan.

Rowe, M. B. (January-February 1986). "Wait Time: Slowing Down May Be a Way of Speeding Up." *The Journal of Teacher Education* 31, 1: 43-50.

Sanders, N. (1966). *Classroom Questions: What Kinds*. New York: Harper and Row.

Slavin, R. (May 1981). "Synthesis of Research on Cooperative Learning." *Educational Leadership* 38, 8: 655-660.

Taba, H. (May 1965). "Teaching of Thinking." *Elementary English* 42, 2: 534.

Taba, H., S. Levine, and F. Elzey. (1964). *Thinking in Elementary School Children*. San Francisco: San Francisco State College, Cooperative Research Project No. 1574.

Walberg, H. J. (September 1986). "What Works in a Nation Still at Risk." *Educational Leadership* 44, 1: 7-10.

Walberg, H. J. (March 1988). "Synthesis of Research on Time and Learning." *Educational Leadership* 45, 6: 76-85.

Wassermann, S. (1988). *The Asking of Wonderful Questions*. Bloomington, Ind.: Phi Delta Kappa.

Widaman, K. F., and S. Kagan. (Winter 1987). "Cooperativeness and Achievement: Interaction of Student Cooperativeness with Cooperative versus Competitive Classroom Organization." *Journal of School Psychology* 25, 4: 355-365.

Raising Student Motivation (Chapters 3, 4, and 5)

Adams, A., and E. L. Bebensee. (1983). *Success in Reading and Writing*. Glenview, Ill.: Good Year.

Akin, T. (1992). *The Best Self-Esteem Activities for the Elementary Grades*. Spring Valley, Calif.: Innerchoice.

Anderson, L. M. (1989). "Classroom Instruction." In *Knowledge Base for the Beginning Teacher*, edited by M. C. Reynolds. New York: Pergamon.

Atkinson, J. W., and J. O. Raynor. (1974). *Motivation and Achievement*. Washington, D.C.: Winston.

Brandt, R., ed. (1989). *Readings from Educational Leadership: Teaching Thinking*. Alexandria, Va.: ASCD.

Brophy, J. E. (1981). "Teacher Praise: A Functional Analysis." Occasional Paper No. 28. East Lansing: Michigan State University Institute for Research on Teaching.

Caine, R., and G. Caine. (1991). *Making Connections: Teaching and the Human Brain*. Alexandria, Va.: ASCD.

Canfield, J. (September 1990). "Improving Students' Self-Esteem." *Educational Leadership* 48, 1: 48-50.

Crump, C. (April 1970). "Teachers, Questions, and Cognition." *Educational Leadership* 27, 7: 657-660.

Cummings, C. (1980). *Teaching Makes a Difference*. Edmonds, Wash.: Teaching Inc.

Cummings, C. (1983). *Managing to Teach*. Edmonds, Wash.: Teaching Inc.

deCharms, R. (1976). *Enhancing Motivation: Change in the classroom*. New York: Irvington.

Deci, E. L. (1978). "Application of Research on the Effect of Rewards." In *The Hidden Costs of Rewards: New Perspectives on the Psychology of Human Motivation*, edited by M. Lepper and D. Greene. Hillsdale, N.J.: Lawrence Erlbaum.

Emmer, E., and C. Everston. (December 1980/January 1981). "Synthesis of Research on Classroom Management." *Educational Leadership* 38, 4: 342-347.

Emmer, E. T. (1988). "Praise and the Instructional Process." *Journal of Classroom Interaction* 23, 2: 32-39.

Gibbs, Jeanne (1987). *Tribes: A Process for Social Development and Cooperative Learning*. Santa Rosa, Calif.: Center Source Publications.

Harmin, M. (1990). *How to Plan a Program for Moral Education*. Alexandria, Va.: ASCD.

Hart, L. (1975). *How the Brain Works*. New York: Basic Books.

Hart, L. (1983). *Human Brain, Human Learning*. New York: Longman.

Hill, P. W., and B. McGraw. (1981). "Testing the Simplex Assumption Underlying Bloom's Taxonomy." *American Educational Research Journal* 18: 93-101.

Hunter, M. C., (1976). *Rx: Improved Instruction*. El Segundo, Calif.: T.I.P. Publications.

Hunter, M., and P. V. Carlson. (1971). *Improving Your Child's Behavior*. Glendale, Calif.: Bowmar.

Johnson, D. W., R. T. Johnson, E. J. Holubec, and P. Roy. (1984). *Circles of Learning: Cooperation in the Classroom*. Alexandria, Va.: ASCD.

Joyce, B., and M. Weil. (1992). *Models of Teaching*. Englewood Cliffs, N.J.: Prentice-Hall.

Keltner, J. W. (1967). *Group Discussion Processes* (p. 113). New York: Longman.

Kindsvetter, R., and W. Wilen. (1989). *Dynamics of Effective Teaching*. New York: Longman.

Kuslan, L. I., and A. H. Stone. (1968). *Teaching Children Science: An Inquiry Approach* (pp. 138-139). Belmont, Calif.: Wadsworth.

Lepper, M., and D. Greene, eds. (1978). *The Hidden Costs of Rewards: New Perspectives on the Psychology of Human Motivation*. Hillsdale, N.J.: Lawrence Erlbaum.

McClelland, D. C., ed. (1985). *Human Motivation*. Glenview, Ill.: Scott Foresman.

Marzano, R. J. (1992). *A Different Kind of Classroom: Teaching with Dimensions of Learning*. Alexandria, Va.: ASCD.

Moorman, C., and N. Moorman. (1989). *Teacher Talk*. Bay City, Mich.: Personal Power Press.

Moorman, C., and D. Dishon. (1983) *Our Classroom: We Can Learn Together*. Bay City, Mich.: Personal Power Press.

Murray, F. B. (1989). "Explanations in Education." In *Knowledge Base for the Beginning Teacher*, edited by M. C. Reynolds. New York: Pergamon.

Nave, B. (December 1990). *Self-Esteem: The Key to Student Success. A Series of Solutions and Strategies. Number 3*. Clemson, S.C.: National Dropout Prevention Center.

Petri, H. L. (1986). *Motivation: Theory and Research*. Belmont, Calif.: Wadsworth.

Pilon, G. H. (1983). *Self-Concept and Reading the Workshop Way*. New Orleans, La.: Workshop Way.

Weiner, B. (1980). *Human Motivation*. New York: Holt, Reinhart and Winston.

Wlodkowski, R. J. (1978). *Motivation and Teaching: A Practical Guide*. Washington, D.C.: National Education Association.

Organizing the Classroom (Chapters 6, 7, 8, and 9)

Aronson, E., N. Blaney, C. Stephan, J. Sikes, and M. Snapp. (1978). *The Jigsaw Classroom*. Beverly Hills, Calif.: Sage.

Bellanca, J., and R. Fogarty. (1990). *Blueprints for Cooperative Learning in the Thinking Classroom*. Palatine, Ill.: Skylight.

Brophy, J. E. (1982). "Supplemental Group Management Techniques." In *Helping Teachers Manage Classrooms*, edited by D. Duke. Alexandria, Va.: ASCD.

Carr, E., and D. Ogle. (April 1987). "K-W-L Plus: A Strategy for Comprehension and Summarization." *Journal of Reading* 30, 7: 626-631.

Cooper, H. M., and D. Tom. (September 1984). "Teacher Expectation Research: A Review with Implications for Classroom Instruction." *Elementary School Journal* 85, 1: 77-89.

Corno, L. (1979). "Classroom Instruction and the Matter of Time." In *Classroom Management, The 78th Yearbook of the National Society for the Study of Education*, edited by D. Duke. Chicago: University of Chicago Press.

Cummings, C. (1980). *Teaching Makes a Difference*. Edmonds, Wash.: Teaching.

Cummings, C. (1983). *Managing to Teach*. Edmonds, Wash.: Teaching Inc.

Emmer, E., and C. Everston. (December 1980/January 1981). "Synthesis of Research on Classroom Management." *Educational Leadership* 38, 4: 342-347.

Evertson, C. (1989). "Classroom Organization and Management." In *Knowledge Base for the Beginning Teacher*, edited by M. C. Reynolds. New York: Pergamon.

Fantuzzo, J. W. (Winter 1990). "An Evaluation of Reciprocal Peer Tutoring Across Elementary School Settings." *Journal of School Psychology* 28, 4: 309-23.

Gabbert, B., D. W. Johnson, and R. Johnson. (1986). "Cooperative Learning, Group-to-Individual Transfer, Process Gain, and the Acquisition of Cognitive Reasoning Strategies." *Journal of Psychology* 120: 265-278.

Good, T. L. (July-August 1987). "Two Decades of Research on Teacher Expectations: Findings and Future Directions." *Journal of Teacher Education* 38, 4: 32-47.

Hoffman, R. W., and R. Plutchik. (1959). *Small-Group Discussions in Orientation and Teaching*. New York: Putnam.

Hunter, M. (1984). "Knowing, Teaching, and Supervising." In *Using What We Know About Teaching*, edited by P. Hosford (1984 Yearbook). Alexandria, Va.: ASCD.

Jackins, H. (1974). *The Human Side of Human Beings*. Seattle, Wash.: Rational Island Publishers.

Johnson, D. W., and R. Johnson. (1987). *Creative Conflict*. Edina, Minn.: Interaction Book

Company.

Johnson, D. W., and R. Johnson. (May 1988). "Critical Thinking Through Structured Controversy." *Educational Leadership* 45, 8: 58-64.

Johnson, D. W., and R. Johnson. (1989). *Cooperation and Competition: Theory and Research.* Edina, Minn.: Interaction Book Company.

Johnson, D. W., R. T. Johnson, E. J. Holubec, and P. Roy. (1984). *Circles of Learning: Cooperation in the Classroom.* Alexandria, Va.: ASCD.

Kagan, S. (December 1989/January 1990). "The Structural Approach to Cooperative Learning." *Educational Leadership* 47, 4: 12-15.

Moorman, C., and D. Dishon. (1983) *Our Classroom: We Can Learn Together.* Englewood Cliffs, N.J.: Prentice-Hall.

Pilon, G. H. (1987). *The Workshop Schedule.* New Orleans, La.: Workshop Way. Note: there are different schedules for different grade levels.

Rosenshine, B. (1970). "Enthusiastic Teaching, A Research Review." *School Review* 78: 279-301.

Rosenshine, B. (1979). "Content, Time and Direct Instruction." In *Research on Teaching,* edited by P. L. Peterson and H. J. Walberg. Berkeley: McCutchan.

Rowe, M. B. (January-February 1986). "Wait Time: Slowing Down May Be a Way of Speeding Up!" *The Journal of Teacher Education* 31, 1: 43-50.

Schmuck, R., and P. Schmuck. (1988). *Group Processes in the Classroom.* 5th ed. Dubuque, Iowa: William C. Brown.

Slavin, R. (May 1981). "Synthesis of Research on Cooperative Learning." *Educational Leadership* 38, 8: 655-660.

Slavin, R. E. (October 1988). "Cooperative Learning and Student Achievement." *Educational Leadership* 46, 2: 31-33.

Slavin, R. E. (February 1991). "Group Rewards Make Groupwork Work." *Educational Leadership* 48, 5: 89-91.

Sharan, Y., and S. Sharan. (December 1989/January 1990). "Group Investigation Expands Cooperative Learning." *Educational Leadership* 47, 4: 17-21.

Taba, H. (1967). *Teachers' Handbook for Elementary Social Studies.* Palo Alto: Addison-Wesley.

Walberg, H. J. (March 1988). "Synthesis of Research on Time and Learning." *Educational Leadership* 45, 6: 76-85.

Widaman, K. F., and S. Kagan. (Winter 1987). "Cooperativeness and Achievement: Interaction of Student Cooperativeness with Cooperative versus Competitive Classroom Organization." *Journal of School Psychology* 25, 4: 355-365.

Wittrock, M. (1986). "Students' Thought Processes." In *Handbook of Research on Teaching,* edited by M. C. Wittrock. New York: Macmillan.

Handling Homework, Testing, and Grading (Chapters 10 and 11)

Annis, L. (1979). "The Processes and Effects of Peer Tutoring." *Human Learning* 2: 39-47.

Biddle, B., and D. S. Anderson (1986). "Theory, Methods, Knowledge, and Research on Teaching." In *Handbook of Research on Teaching,* edited by M. C. Wittrock. New York: Macmillan.

Camp, R. (Spring 1990). "Thinking Together About Portfolios." *National Writing Project and the Center for the Study of Writing and Literacy* 12, 2: 8-14, 27.

Channon, G. (1970). *Homework.* New York: Outerbridge.

Cooper, H. (1989). *Homework.* New York: Longman.

Cooper, H. M. (1989). *Integrating Research: A Guide for Literature Reviews.* 2nd ed. Newbury Park, Calif.: Sage.

Farnan, N., and R. Kelly. (July-September 1991). "Keeping Track: Creating Assessment Portfolios in Reading and Writing." *Quarterly of the National Writing Project and the Center for the Study of Writing and Literacy* 14, 1: 14-17.

Herber, H. L. (1978). *Teaching Reading in the Content Areas,* 2nd ed. Englewood Cliffs, N.J.: Prentice-Hall.

Herman, J., P. Aschbacher, and L. Winters. (1992). *A Practical Guide to Alternative Assessment.* Alexandria, Va.: ASCD.

Knight, P. (May 1992). "How I Use Portfolios in Mathematics." *Educational Leadership* 49, 8: 71-72.

McDaniel, T. (1979). "Designing Essay Questions for Different Levels of Learning." *Improving College and University Teaching* 27, 3: 120-123.

Moore, M. R. (1967). "A Proposed Taxonomy of the Perceptual Domain and Some Suggested Applications." Test Development Report 67-3. Princeton, N.J.: Educational Testing Service.

National Commission on Excellence in Education. (1983). *A Nation at Risk: The Imperative for Educational Reform.* Washington D.C.: U.S. Department of Education.

Olson, M. W. (January-March 1991). "Portfolios: Education Tools (Research into Practice)." *Reading Psychology* 12, 1: 73-80.

Richards, J. (1982). "Homework." In *Encyclopedia of Educational Research,* 5th ed., edited by H. E. Mitzel, J. Hardin Best, and W. Rabinowitz. New York: Macmillan.

Roe, M. F. (December 1991). *Portfolios: From Mandate to Implementation.* Paper presented at the Annual Meeting of the National Reading Conference, Palm Springs, Calif.

Roettger, D., and M. Szymczuk, eds. (1990). *Guide for Developing Student Portfolios.* Draft version. Johnston, Iowa: Heartland Area Education Agency 11.

Tierney, R. J. (1991). *Portfolio Assessment in the Reading-Writing Classroom.* Norwood, Mass.: Christopher-Gordon Publishers.

Trachtenberg, D. (1974). "Student Tasks in Text Materials: What Cognitive Skills Do They Tap?" *Peabody Journal of Education* 52, 1: 54-57.

Walberg, H. J. (April 1985). "Homework's Powerful Effects on Learning." *Educational Leadership* 42, 7: 76-79.

Wolf, D. P. (December 1987/January 1988). "Opening Up Assessment." *Educational Leadership* 45, 4: 24-29.

Wolf, D. P. (April 1989). "Portfolio Assessment: Sampling Student Work." *Educational Leadership* 46, 7: 35-39.

Producing Meaningful Learning (Chapters 12, 13, and 14)

Anderson L. (1989). "Implementing Instructional Programs to Promote Meaningful, Self-regulated Learning." In *Advances in Research on Teaching. Vol 1: Teaching for Meaningful Understanding and Self-regulated Learning,* edited by J. Brophy. Greenwich, Conn.: JAI.

Applebee, A. (1986). "Problems in Process Approaches: Toward a Reconceptualization of Process Instruction." In *The Teaching of Writing* (85th yearbook of the National Society for the Study of Education), edited by A. Petrosky and D. Bartholomae. Chicago: University of Chicago Press.

Bailis, P., and M. Hunter. (August 1985). "Do Your Words Get Them to Think?" *Learning* 14, 1: 43.

Belch, Jean. (1974). *Contemporary Games, Vol. I: Directory* and *Vol. II: Bibliography.* Detroit: Gale Research Co.

Bloom, B. S. (1976). *Human Characteristics and School Learning.* New York: McGraw-Hill.

Bloom, B., and D. R. Krathwohl. (1977; reprint of 1956 edition). *Taxonomy of Educational Objectives, Handbook I: Cognitive Domain.* New York: David McKay Company.

Brandt, R. (September 1984). "Teaching Of Thinking, For Thinking, About Thinking." *Educational Leadership* 42, 1: 3.

Brandt, R., ed. (1989). *Readings from Educational Leadership: Teaching Thinking.* Alexandria, Va.: ASCD.

Brandt, R. (December 1992/January 1993). "On Outcome-Based Education: A Conversation with Bill Spady." *Educational Leadership* 50, 4: 66-71.

Brophy, J. (1989). *Advances in Research on Teaching. Vol.I: Teaching for Meaningful Understanding and Self-regulated Learning.* Greenwich, Conn.: JAI.

Brown, M. A. S. (1977). "Games Can Make You a Winning Teacher." *Forecast* 23: 19.

Bruner, J. S., and M. J. Kenny. (1966). *Studies in Cognitive Growth.* New York: John Wiley and Sons.

Bruner, J. S., J. J. Goodnow, and G. A. Austin. (1956). *A Study of Thinking.* New York: John Wiley and Sons.

Calkins, L. (1986). *The Art of Teaching Writing.* Exeter: Heinemann.

Carr, E., and D. Ogle. (April 1987). "K-W-L Plus: A Strategy for Comprehension and Summarization." *Journal of Reading* 30, 7: 626-631.

Cazden, C., and H. Mehan. (1989) "Principles from Sociology and Anthropology: Context, Code, Classroom and Culture." In *Knowledge Base for the Beginning Teacher,* edited by M. C. Reynolds. New York: Pergamon.

Christenbury, L., and P. P. Kelly. (1983). "Questioning: A Critical Path to Critical Thinking" (Public Domain Document NIE 400-78-0026, p. 4). Urbana, Ill.: ERIC Clearinghouse on Reading and Communications Skills and the National Council of Teachers of English.

Costa, A. L., ed. (1991). *Developing Minds: A Resource Book for Teaching Thinking* and *Programs for Teaching Thinking.* Revised ed., vols. 1 and 2. Alexandria, Va.: ASCD.

Costa, A., and L. Lowrey. (1989). *Techniques for Teaching Thinking.* Pacific Grove, Calif.: Midwest Publications.

Cummings, C. (1983). *Managing to Teach.* Edmonds, Wash.: Teaching Inc.

Feldhusen, J, R. Ames, and K. Linden. (1974). "Designing Instruction to Achieve Higher Level Goals and Objectives." *Educational Technology* 14, 10: 21-23.

Flavell, J. H. (1976). "Metacognitive Aspects of Problem Solving." In *The Nature of Intelligence,* edited by L. B. Resnick. Hillsdale, N.J.: Lawrence Erlbaum.

Gabbert, B., D. W. Johnson, and R. Johnson. (1986). "Cooperative Learning, Group-to-Individual Transfer, Process Gain, and the Acquisition of Cognitive Reasoning Strategies." *Journal of Psychology* 120: 265-278.

Gall, M. (December 1970). "The Use of Questions in Teaching." *Review of Educational Research* 40, 5: 207-220.

Gordon, A. K. (1972). *Games for Growth.* Palo Alto, Calif.: Science Research Associates, Inc.

Grossman, P., S. M. Wilson, and L. S. Shulman. (1989). "Teachers of Substance: Subject Matter Knowledge for Teaching." In *Knowledge Base for the Beginning Teacher,* edited by M. C. Reynolds. New York: Pergamon.

Heiman, M., and J. Slomianko, eds. (1987). *Thinking Skills Instruction: Concepts and Techniques.* Building Students' Thinking Skills series. Washington, D.C.: National Education Association.

Johnson, D., and R. Johnson. (1975). *Learning Together and Alone.* Englewood Cliffs, N.J.: Prentice-Hall.

Johnson, D. W., and R. Johnson. (1989). *Cooperation and Competition: Theory and Research.* Edina, Minn.: Interaction Book Company.

Johnson, D., R. Johnson, P. Roy, and E. J. Holubec. (1984). *Circles of Learning: Cooperation in the Classroom.* Alexandria, Va.: ASCD.

Kagan, S. (1980). "Cooperation-Competition, Culture, and Structural Bias in Classrooms." In *Cooperation in Education,* edited by S. Sharan, P. Hare, C. Webb, and R. Hertz-Lazarowitz. Provo, Utah: Brigham Young University Press.

Marzano, R. J. (1992). *A Different Kind of Classroom: Teaching with Dimensions of Learning.* Alexandria, Va.: ASCD.

Marzano, R. J., R. S. Brandt, C. S. Hughes, B. F. Jones, B. Z. Presseisen, and S. C. Rankin. (1988). *Dimensions of Thinking: A Framework for Curriculum and Instruction.* Alexandria,

Va.: ASCD.

Newmann, F. (1988). *Higher Order Thinking in High School Social Studies: An Analysis of Classrooms, Teachers, Students, and Leadership.* Madison: University of Wisconsin, National Center for Effective Secondary Schools.

Nucci, L. (1989). "Knowledge of the Learner: The Development of Children's Concepts of Self, Morality and Societal Convention." In *Knowledge Base for the Beginning Teacher,* edited by M. C. Reynolds. New York: Pergamon.

Ogle, D. (1986). "K-W-L: A Teaching Model That Develops Active Reading of Expository Text." *The Reading Teacher* 39:564-576.

Pilon, G. H. (1981a). *Thinkers for Grade 3.* New Orleans, La.: Workshop Way.

Pilon, G. H. (1981b). *Thinkers for Grade 4.* New Orleans, La.: Workshop Way.

Pilon, G. H. (1984a). *Primary Thinkers for Kindergarten and First Grade.* New Orleans, La.: Workshop Way.

Pilon, G. H. (1984b). *Thinkers for Grade 5.* New Orleans, La.: Workshop Way.

Pilon, G. H. (1986). *English Thinkers for Junior High.* New Orleans, La.: Workshop Way.

Pilon, G. H. (1988). *Math Thinkers for Junior High.* New Orleans, La.: Workshop Way.

Pinnell, G., and D. Deford. (1988). *Reading Recovery: Early Intervention for At Risk First Graders.* Arlington, Va.: Educational Research Service.

Redfield, D., and E. Rousseau. (Summer 1981). "A Meta-Analysis on Teacher Questioning Behavior." *Review of Educational Research* 51: 234-245.

Resnick, L. (1987). *Education and Learning to Think.* Washington, D.C.: National Academy Press.

Rosaen, C. (1989). "Writing in the Content Areas: Researching Its Potential in the Learning Process." In *Advances in Research on Teaching. Vol I: Teaching for Meaningful Understanding and Self-regulated Learning.* Greenwich, Conn.: JAI.

Rosenshine, B. (1976). "Classroom Instruction." In *Psychology of Teaching, 77th Yearbook of the National Study of Education,* edited by N. Gage. Chicago: University of Chicago Press.

Sharan, Y., and S. Sharan. (December 1989/January 1990). "Group Investigation Expands Cooperative Learning." *Educational Leadership* 47, 4: 17-21.

Slavin, R. E. (April 1989). "On Mastery Learning and Mastery Teaching." *Educational Leadership* 46, 7: 77-79.

Slavin, R. (May 1981). "Synthesis of Research on Cooperative Learning." *Educational Leadership* 38, 8: 655-660.

Strike, K. A. (1975). "The Logic of Learning by Discovery." *Review of Educational Research* 45, 3: 461-483.

Taba, H. (May 1965). "Teaching of Thinking." *Elementary English* 42, 2: 534.

Taba, H., S. Levine, and F. Elzey. (1964). *Thinking in Elementary School Children.* San Francisco, Calif.: San Francisco State College, Cooperative Research Project No. 1574.

Van Manen, M. (1977). "Linking Ways of Knowing with Ways of Being Practical." *Curriculum Inquiry* 6, 3: 205-228.

Vye, N. J., and J. D. Bransford. (October 1981). "Programs for Teaching Thinking." *Educational Leadership* 39: 26-28.

Wassermann, S. (1991). *Serious Players: Empowering Children in the Primary Grades.* New York: Teachers College Press.

Wassermann, S., and G. Ivany. (1988). *Teaching Elementary Science: Who's Afraid of Spiders?* New York: Harper Row.

Whimbey, A. (April 1980). "Students Can Learn to Be Better Problem Solvers." *Educational Leadership* 37, 7: 560-565.

Whimbey, A., and J. Lochhead. (1986). *Problem Solving and Comprehension.* Hillsdale, N.J.: Lawrence Erlbaum.

Index/Glossary

DESCA challenges. Challenges that stretch students' capacity to live with full dignity, high energy, wise self-management, in respectful community, or with open awareness (DESCA). Strategy 5.4, page 84

DESCA inspirations. Teacher comments to stir appreciation of the inherent *dignity* of all students; appropriate personal *energy*; intelligent *self-management*; healthful *community* relationships; and searching, open *awareness*. Strategy 4.9, page 74

Focus-on-learning statement. Explaining that the focus in the class is on learning, not on grading, and inviting students to adjust accordingly. Strategy 11.3, page 148

Grading plan. A plan for grading that considers both the teacher's current grading responsibilities and the students' long-term welfare. Strategy 11.2, page 145

Guided practice. Students practicing a skill with teacher guidance, so students gradually move toward excellence. Strategy 2.13, page 44

Hand-raising signal. The teacher raises a hand to signal the end of small-group discussion; students who see the hand then raise their own hand. Hands stay raised until all discussion has ceased. Strategy 8.8, page 116

High expectations. Maintaining an expectation that students will do excellent work, even there is not yet evidence that they will do so. Strategy 5.3, page 82

Homework hearing. A teacher meeting briefly with each student to hear about completed homework. Strategy 10.3, page 137

Homework sharing groups. Groups (usually pairs) of students who sit together to review or correct homework. Strategy 10.2, page 135

Homework unlike classwork. Homework assignments distinctly different from classroom activities. Strategy 10.4, page 141

Honest delight. A statement expressing spontaneous delight with a student. Strategy 4.8, page 72

"I appreciate" message. A statement that communicates something honestly appreciated about students. Strategy 4.1, page 63

Immediate work assignment. Work students handle as soon as they enter the classroom. Strategy 6.2, page 88

"I'm with you" message. A message that communicates an empathetic acceptance or understanding of a student. Strategy 4.2, page 64

Inspiring statement. A statement that cheers students on to do their best work. Strategy 5.2, page 81

Intelligence call up. Reminders that inspire students to call up and exercise their natural human intelligence. Strategy 9.1, page 118

"I say" review. Pairs of students sharing what they have to say about a certain subject. Strategy 12.2, page 156

Learning challenge. An assignment posed as a challenge or an opportunity, not as a chore or burden. Strategy 5.1, page 78

Learning pairs. Students working in pairs to help each other learn. Strategy 12.1, page 155

Lesson agreement. Outlining the lesson planned and inviting student agreement. Strategy 6.1, page 87

Like/might review. Students reviewing their recent behavior, noting what they *liked* about it and what they *might* do differently another time. Strategy 7.1, page 92

Limited variety. Variety in a classroom sufficient to keep students involved, yet not so diverse as to threaten students' security and need for predictability. Strategy 1.4, page 21

Make a prediction. Asking students to think ahead and make predictions. Strategy 13.6, page 165

Motivating question. A question focusing student attention and inspiring student thinking. Strategy 6.3, page 89

New or good invitation. Inviting a class to share events in their lives that are new or good. Strategy 6.4, page 89

Nod of recognition. A nod to a student that indicates the teacher is aware the student has volunteered. Strategy 9.3, page 122

Once principle. Announcing that directions will be given only once and that students needing help are to use their intelligence and find an appropriate way to catch up. Strategy 9.4, page 122

Option display. Small groups work on a problem, aiming to construct a display that shows several options for solving the problem, the likely consequences of each option, and the group's best overall recommendation. Strategy 8.3, page 105

Outcome sentences. Sentences students write after reflecting on a lesson or experience, prompted by such phrases as I learned . . . , I'm beginning to wonder . . . , I was surprised . . . Strategy 2.3, page 25

Paired reading. Pairs of students take turns reading aloud to each other. Strategy 8.1, page 101

Pass the Q&A. The teacher announcing a question and an answer and all students passing the question and answer along, with one student asking the question, the next answering it. Strategy 12.3, page 157

Plain corrects. Straightforwardly informing a student that an answer is correct and then moving on. Strategy 4.4, page 67

Plain incorrects. Straightforwardly informing a student that an answer is not correct and then moving on. Strategy 4.5, page 68

Portfolio. A collection of student work. Strategy 11.1, page 143

Praise and rewards for all. Praise or rewards offered to the group as a whole. Strategy 4.7, page 71

Project work. Students working on a task for an extended time period, alone or in small groups, usually to produce a tangible product. Strategy 8.6, page 110

Question, all write. Students each writing an answer to a question before the teacher calls on one student or announces the correct answer. Strategy 2.2, page 24

Quick pace. A classroom pace fast enough to keep all students actively involved and prevent students' attention from wandering. Strategy 1.2, page 18

Report card plan. Planning to handle report cards in a way responsive both to professional requirements and the best interests of students. Strategy 11.4, page 152

Review test. The teacher asking a series of questions about prior material, all students writing an answer to each question, and the teacher announcing the correct answer, either orally or in writing, after each question. Strategy 2.14, page 46

Risk reminder. Reminding students that learning often involves risks, with perhaps some encouragement to consider risking in class today. Strategy 6.5, page 90

Set of speakers. Requesting volunteers to speak and then, from all volunteers, choosing a set of students who will have a turn. Strategy 9.2, page 121

Sharing pairs. Students pairing up and sharing thoughts. Strategy 2.7, page 32

Silent response. Making a mental note of a student error or problem, but leaving until later the consideration of what, if anything, is to be done about it. Strategy 4.6, page 69

Solve a problem. Asking students to solve a problem that lacks an obvious solution. Strategy 13.8, page 167

Sort the items. Students placing items into categories specified by the teacher. Strategy 13.1, page 161

Speak-write. A lecture procedure containing occasional pauses that students know are for writing personal reactions, a summary of what they heard, questions, or anything else students choose. Strategy 2.10, page 38

Student procedure mastery. Spending enough time teaching classroom procedures so students will be able to follow them easily and efficiently. Strategy 9.7, page 129

Support group. Several students, usually a group of four, who regularly sit together and offer appropriate support to one another. Strategy 8.5, page 109

Task and team skill group. A small group of students working at a task and simultaneously practicing an interpersonal skill. Strategy 8.7, page 114

Task group, share group. Students considering a problem in small task groups and then regrouping so each student can share task-group work with students who were in different task groups. Strategy 8.2, page 102

Teaching in layers, not lumps. Returning to topics from time to time, rather than aiming for mastery at any one time, so learnings are reinforced over time and the risk of losing student involvement is minimized. Strategy 1.3, page 20

Think aloud. Talking aloud while working through a problem. Strategy 2.12, page 42

Thought/feel cards. Notes students make, usually anonymously, of personal thoughts or feelings currently in their awareness. Strategy 7.2, page 93

Truth signs. Posted signs that remind students of important truths about learning and living. Strategy 3.1, page 49

Tutor training. Lessons teaching students skills for effectively giving and receiving help. Strategy 9.6, page 124

Underexplain with learning pairs. Explaining material briefly, so that only some students fully understand it, and then asking pairs to work together to help each other learn the material. Strategy 2.4, page 27

Voting. Asking questions to which students can respond nonverbally, as by asking, "How many of you . . . ?" Strategy 2.5, page 30

What I know, what I want to know (or K-W-L). In preparation for study, asking students to note what they already know about a topic and what they might want to know about it. Strategy 14.4, page 178

What might explain? Asking students to consider what might explain an event. Strategy 13.7, page 166

What's the difference? Asking students how two or more items differ. Strategy 13.3, page 163

What's the same? Asking students how two or more items are the same. Strategy 13.4, page 164

Whip around, pass option. Asking each student in turn to speak to an issue or to say "I pass." Strategy 2.1, page 23

Write a summary. Asking students to write a summary of information. Strategy 13.5, page 165

Current ASCD Networks

ASCD sponsors numerous networks that help members exchange ideas, share common interests, identify and solve problems, grow professionally, and establish collegial relationships. The following networks may be of particular interest to readers of this book:

Brain-Based Education/Learning Styles. *Contact:* Joan Caulfield, Coordinator, Coll./Schl. Rel., Rockhurst College, 1100 Rockhurst Rd., Kansas City, MO 64110. TEL (816) 926-4140 FAX (816) 926-4588. Also, Wayne Jennings, Inst./Learning & Teaching, 2550 University, Rm. 347N, St. Paul, MN 55114-1052. TEL (612) 645-0200.

Character Education. *Contact:* Kevin Ryan, Director, Center for the Advancement of Ethics & Character, School of Education, Boston University, 605 Commonwealth Ave. Room 356, Boston, MA 02215. TEL (617) 353-3262 FAX (617) 353-3924.

Cooperative Learning. *Contact:* Harlan Rimmerman, Director, N. Kansas City School District, 2000 N.E. 46th St., Kansas City, MO 64116. TEL (816) 453-5050.

Dimensions of Learning. *Contact:* Frances Jones, Executive Director, Piedmont Triad Horizons Education Consortium, School of Education, University of North Carolina, Greensboro, NC 27412-5001. TEL (919) 334-5100, x301 FAX (919) 334-4093.

Teaching Thinking. *Contact:* Esther Fusco, Principal & Director of Curriculum, Port Jefferson School District, 24 Hopewell Dr., Stony Brook, NY 11790. TEL (516) 473-8710 FAX (516) 928-0293.

Wholistic Education. *Contact:* John Palladino, Associate Professor of Education, Long Island University, C.W. Post Campus, Brookville, NY 11548. TEL (516) 299-2372 or 299-2374 FAX (516) 626-2476.

Networks Program Liaison: Susan K. Nicklas, Director, Field Services, ASCD, 1250 N. Pitt St., Alexandria, VA 22314-1453. TEL (703) 549-9110, x500 FAX (703) 549-3891.